Luisa Piccarreta

D0943109

When the Divine Will Reigns in Souls

—Book of Heaven—

A Selection of Passages

This is the first English Edition
translated from the Spanish version titled:
"La Divina Voluntad Obrante En Las Criaturas"

The Spanish Editions contain the full texts of
Volumes 13 and 14 of Luisa Piccarreta's Writings.
They are not included in this English Version, being
available separately.

†

Ricardo Guizar Diaz
Bishop of Atlacomulco

To make her writings known, the friends of Luisa
Piccarreta present this publication of selected paragraphs.
Once, again, thanks should be given to my good friend, José
Luis Acuña.

I believe the writings of Luisa can inspire many souls to a
much more generous adhesion to the Divine Will. This was
the attitude that Luisa lived so intensely and profoundly. This
was the attitude that the Most Holy Virgin Mary offered to
God when pronouncing her "Fiat" — "Let it be done." It is the
same attitude with which Jesus accepted and lived his Most
Holy Passion. Also, it is the same attitude He wanted us to
learn and have in our prayer and in our lives when He taught
us the "Our Father": "May your Will be done on earth as It is
in Heaven."

May this same Jesus deign, through his Holy Spirit, to
hasten many souls through the longing to fully conform their
lives to the Divine Will so that "rooted and cemented in his
Love, we might grow in every manner toward Him who is the
Head, Christ" (Ef. 4,5).

Atlacomulco, Mexico - November 22, 1992

＋ Ricardo Guizar Diaz
Obispo de Atlacomulco

...and finally the dawn

The year 1994 has been extraordinarily important for the Cause (Process of Beatification) of Luisa and the triumph of the Reign of the Divine Will in the world. The Sacred Congregation of the Faith (Ex Santo Oficio) informed the Sacred Congregation responsible for the Causes of Saints that there was no objection in initiating the Cause of Luisa. ...What is certain is that the Providence of God and the prayers of so many have resulted in the Church's interest in Luisa whose life and testimony show an immense generosity. Accordingly, on Holy Saturday, April 3, 1994, the Archbishop of Trani, the Diocese in which Luisa lived, announced that the Sacred Congregation for the Causes of Saints had informed him that the Cause for the Beatification of Luisa could begin. In the following months a canonical commission was formed to begin the preliminary informative process. As a result, on November 20, 1994, on the Solemnity of Christ the King in the Church of Luisa's baptism, his Excellency Archishop Carmelo Cassati read the Edict to officially open the Cause of Beatification in which he requested that Luisa's personal objects or testimonies be presented to either him or the Postulator in charge of her writings.

The words which the prelate used in speaking about Luisa were precious: "...a victim soul, who offered herself out of love and enormous generosity to accompany Jesus in his Passion, living it in bed for more than sixty years. Only in the light of her cross, entering into the spiritual situation in which she offered herself, can one penetrate her doctrine and message without distorting it or changing it to frivolous philosophical works, deforming it and modifying it toward grave doctrinal errors and conduct."

Let us give thanks to God because, finally, Holy Mother Church has begun to take in her hands the Fruit of her Tree, the first fruits of her Kingdom, to know and savor it. "How wonderful it is to see a messenger coming across the mountain, bringing good news, the news of peace and salvation to Zion. Do you hear? Those who guard the city are shouting together for joy, because they see with their own eyes the return of the Lord of Zion (Is. 52, 7-8).

Fr. Pablo Martin

Luisa Piccarreta

From time to time it has pleased God to bring about monumental and universal changes in the affairs of mankind. When these events occur it has been the usual way with our God to give us very special persons to be identified in a particular manner with these changes.

In the beginning when the *Decree of Creation* brought the human race into existence, **Adam and Eve** were chosen to be the first humans to be inserted into time. They were our first parents in the order of nature. Later, humanity had grown so steeped in evil that God saw fit to send the **Great Flood**. He chose **Noah** to build the ark and lead a tiny remnant through that awesome change in human affairs. When the chosen people, the Jews, were to be lead out of the land of Egypt, God chose **Moses**, through whom we were given the Ten Commandments. Centuries later, the **Decree of Redemption** was fulfilled; and the **Only-Begotten of the Father, Jesus,** became Incarnate in the most pure womb of **Mary.** She became the Mother of God, Mother of the Redeemer and cooperated perfectly with Him for the Redemption of mankind.

And now, today, as we approach the end of the Second Millennium of Christianity, humanity has once again degenerated into a most squalid state of evil. The signs are everywhere that a major change is about to take place by the hand of our God. A great purification seems imminent and a New Era is about to dawn upon the earth. This New Era is the realization of the *Decree of Sanctification*, which is the fulfillment of Our Lord's prayer to Our Father that his Kingdom **Come** and that his Will be done on earth **as** It is in Heaven.

The Holy Trinity has chosen another very special person on earth in order to begin this New Era and to show us *how* God's

Will is done in Heaven so that we *(with the Gift of the Divine Will)* can also do It in that same, most sublime manner of Heaven — Here on earth. The name of this very special person is **Luisa Piccarreta**, to whom Our Lord gave many titles pertaining to her extraordinary mission, among which are: *"The Herald of the Reign of the Divine Will," "The First of the Second Generation of the Sons and Daughters of Light," "The Secretary and Scribe of Jesus," "The Little Newborn in the Divine Will," "The Teacher of the Most Sublime Science," and "The Little Daughter of the Divine Will."* This last title is engraved on her tombstone located inside her parish Church, St. Mary the Greek, in Corato, Italy.

As the chosen Herald of the Reign of the Divine Will on earth, Luisa was the Pioneer 'par excellent' to begin this New Era in which Our Father is to receive his greatest Glory. Luisa, who was confined to bed for 64 years without food or water and scarcely any sleep, had little more than a first grade education; but Jesus would come to her every day and illuminate her mind with the most sublime mysteries about God and his Divine Will, which she faithfully wrote down on paper. These writings, done <u>*only in obedience*</u> to her Archbishop through the Priests assigned as her Confessors, comprised a book of 36 Volumes, written over a period of 40 years. This book would become known by the Title that Our Lord Himself gave to it:

"The Kingdom of the FIAT in the Midst of Creatures
Book of Heaven
The Call to the Creature to Return to the Order, the Place, and the Purpose for which it was Created by God"

Thomas M. Fahy

*   *   *

Brief Introduction

"Everything That Christ Lived Enables Us To Live It In Him And That He Live It In Us."

. . .

And this is the purpose of our lives: **To Live In Christ What He Himself Lived And Allow Him To Live It In Us.** Everything else — sacraments, prayers, fasting, mortification, penance — are **Means** to achieve this end. And if they fail, being rendered less efficacious, it is because we fail to permit their complete fecundity.

The writings of Luisa bring us precisely to this point: to repeat in us the same life of Jesus. They bring us because they permit us to **Know** about the interior **Life** of Jesus. They allow us to know how his Divine Will worked with his human will as true God and true man and how everything in him was completed, having been **Lived** in his Divine Will. Working together with his human will, his Divine Will became the depository of all his acts. And everything that Jesus did remained in his Divine Will — in his Divine Volition — waiting that we, living in the Divine Will, find **All The Acts That He Did Throughout His Life** so that they would become our **Life** and the **Life** of each and everyone of our acts. This is to say that Jesus reveals in these writings **His Human And Divine Interior Activity So That We Might Know And Penetrate More Profoundly What He Lived** and, knowing it, we want it and are able to **Live It Ourselves.**

Let us take, for example, this passage: "My daughter, the true life of the soul in my Will is nothing other than the formation of her life in Mine; it is to give my same likeness to everything the soul does. I did nothing other than put in flight in my Divine Will all the internal and external acts I did. I put in flight every thought of my Mind which, flying over every thought of the creature, crowned every human intelligence and carried to my Father's Majesty the homage, adoration, glory, love and reparation for every created thought. This can also be said of my glances, words, movements, heartbeats, footsteps, as well as everything else. Now to live in my Will, the soul should give to herself the activity of my Mind, the manner of my glances, my words, my movements, my heartbeats, my steps. In this way the soul loses her own form and assumes mine. And it does nothing other than give continuous death to herself and continuous life to the Divine Will within. This will repeat my Life in the soul with all the riches It contains, with all my ways, with my merits, with my same Sanctity, with my same Power. Only my Will living in the soul implants in her, in her acts, all the Good and the Life of my acts, doing with the creature a single thing, living a single Life, Mine in her..."

Thus, the more we know **What Christ Lived, The More We Want Him To Live That Life In Us, And The More He Will Be Able To Live It In Us** to the fullness He lived It, in as far as it is possible to the creature.

To form this Divine Life in us, we need the Divine Maternity to make It fruitful: the Holy Virgin Mother who with respect to her mission and maternal office, will make It grow and develop to Its fullness, until we truly become the "image and likeness of the Incarnate Word." All of this is, in essence, the great and preeminent theme of these writings.

* * *

More about
Luisa Piccarreta

...Luisa lived eighty-two years, sixty-four of which she spent in the "smallest cell in the world" – her bed. Over and around the four sides of her bed there was a light metal structure from which hung curtains making her bed a cloister of scarcely two square meters. This was sufficient for her and her Loved One, Jesus, who almost daily visited and taught her so that she would model all her interior being to his likeness. There was space not only for Him, but also for "Mamma" (Blessed Mother), as Luisa called her. The Most Holy Virgin also frequently visited her with the same intentions of making Luisa a perfect copy of the interior of Jesus and her own. Luisa was continuously under the authority of Lady Obedience to which she always submitted and acquiesced. This obedience was imposed by her Confessor, but ultimately originated from her Bishop.

Our Lord intervened to place Luisa decisively and unquestionably in her state as a victim of reparation. The cholera epidemic of 1886, which accounted for many deaths in the region of Corato, was instrumental in her acceptance of the victim state. Jesus asked her to accept a state of suffering to end the scourge and, having accepted, Luisa suffered for three days after which the cholera stopped, even though it had continued to progress for months.

When Luisa was twenty-one years old, her new Confessor, Don Michele de Benedictis, in order to know, test and discern her spirit, imposed as a primary consideration that if she was to suffer, it should be done only through an act of obedience.

A year later, Jesus asked her to offer herself in suffering. But this suffering was not to be intermittent as in the past, but continuous. All her suffering was to make reparation to the Divine Justice, excessively angered, and avert many chastisements for man. These were the chastisements which mankind increasingly merited and which were about to occur. Luisa informed her Confessor of Jesus' wish and asked him to place her under obedience so she could suffer "for a certain time," what she thought would be forty days. Her Confessor gave permission and Luisa remained permanently bed-ridden without EVER being sick[1] or having bed sores. This victim state initiated a new series of singular graces. Jesus visited her very frequently, preparing her for a Mystical Marriage, taking her to perfect conformity with the Divine Will. Jesus continued preparing her for other mystical unions such as the union of the Cross. And one morning, showing Himself as the Crucified Savior, He gave her the most painful stigmata of his Passion. But, responding to her wishes, He left them invisible, having no external manifestations. From that time, she suffered the pains of the Crucifixion which Jesus Himself renewed in her. Luisa, consumed by an insatiable hunger to suffer, had to learn years later that all her desires — wanting to suffer and even wanting to visibly see Jesus — had to yield to the Divine Will.

In 1899, upon the death of her Confessor, a new Confessor, Don Gennaro di Gennaro, assumed responsibility for her care for the next twenty-four years. And as a primary directive, he placed her under obedience and requested she write everything that had happened between her and Jesus since the beginning. She began to write in February of 1899.

Jesus continued preparing Luisa for her sublime mission: the greatest Grace and superior state — to live in the Divine Will. In the year 1900 He spoke to her for the first time about this and gave her the Grace of all graces and designated her as the "Little Daughter of the Divine Will." And with her, in silence and obscurity, our Lord issued in the new Era of Grace, the true **Reign Of The Divine Will On Earth And The Fulfillment Of The Our Father:** may Your Will be done on earth as It is in Heaven **(Fiat Voluntas Tua, Sicut In Coelo Et In Terra)**.

Luisa continued to write thirty-six volumes on the doctrine of living in the Divine Will as well as other works such as the "Hours of

---

[1] Only at the very end of her life did Luisa suffer any natural illness. At that time she was stricken with pneumonia and died fifteen days later on March 4,1947.

the Passion," five editions of which were published in 1915, 1916, 1917, 1921, and 1932 and the "Queen of Heaven in the Reign of the Divine Will," three editions of which were published in 1932, 1933 and 1937. All these works received Nihil Obstats and Imprimaturs. The directive to write under obedience was eventually rescinded and the last chapter of Volume 36 was written on December 28, 1938.

Father Gennaro died in 1922 and was succeeded by Canon D. Francesco De Benedictus who died four years later, in 1926. Her last Confessor named by her Archbishop was Canon D. Benedetto Calvi who attended Luisa until her death.

Finally, on the March 4, 1947, at six o'clock in the morning, Luisa died, having experienced a brief but intense pneumonia. After four days of public veneration of her remains, she received her first honor: her triumphant funeral in which participated many representatives from the Church in Trani, the diocese in which Corato is located, as well as other areas. This is verified through various photographs taken at that time. Today her body rests, with ecclesiastical approval, in the Church of St. Mary the Greek in Corato.

What was a usual day like in the life of Luisa? Her last Confessor, Fr. Benedetto Calvi, has left this testimony:

EXTRAORDINARY PHENOMENA IN HER LIFE

About six o'clock in the morning, the Confessor arrived at her bedside. Luisa was like a block of marble, so strongly contracted that when her sister or some other person of the house tried to sit her up in bed in her usual position to comply with obedience to the Confessor or Bishop, they were incapable of moving her because of the weight. It was as though she were a great block of lead, and they were unable to extend any member of her body due to a strong rigidity. Only when the Confessor (or any Priest if there were special circumstances) gave his benediction and made the sign of the cross on the back of her hand with his thumb, would her life and bodily movements be restored. Only then did she revive and begin to move, allowing her sister to raise and easily place her in her accustomed sitting position.

Another extraordinary phenomenon (already indicated): confined to her bed for sixty-four years, she never suffered any bed sores. Still another extraordinary fact: What was her nourishment? The little she ate was completely returned, resulting in a total abstinence from the time she became bedridden until she died sixty-four years later. Her only food was the Divine Will and Jesus in Holy Communion.

These and other extraordinary phenomena could be observed and meticulously controlled. Moreover, more than a few doctors and professors of Dogmatic, Moral, Ascetic and Mystical Theology, appointed by our diocesan superiors, submitted her to extensive examinations to render a judgment. I mention two of them: Doctor P. Domenico Franze, O.F.M., Professor of Physiology and Medicine at the International University of Rome, and Dr. P. Consalvo Valls, O.F.M., who, himself, is a doctor in Moral, Ascetic and Mystical Theology, as well as others.

After being awoken by her Confessor or some other Priest, Holy Mass was celebrated in her small room at her bedside. Then, after receiving Holy Communion, Luisa remained in ecstasy as though asleep, in intimate conversation with our Lord for two or three hours. She did this without rigidity or loss of her senses. Many times, however, our Blessed Lord was with her during the day in a more noticeable manner such that those around her witnessed it.

When she became conscious, she would sit and begin working in her bed. She sewed and made lace, knitting fine works which were generally ornaments and table cloths, as well as other artifacts for the church.

Each day some young girls and children would gather around her, and she would teach them to make these things; but, more than this, they were attracted by her sweet and natural charm from which emanated the presence of God. Most of the time they were with Luisa in prayer and meditation of the "Hours of the Passion" as Luisa was accustomed to do them. And many of these young girls came to know the "Hours of the Passion" by memory. They made holy hours of reparation and performed other exercises of piety. Her life always appeared exteriorly like that, always the same: work, silence and prayer.

Around 2:30 or 3 o'clock in the afternoon, a small portion of food was given her and after a few minutes, as was already stated, it was returned to a container provided for that purpose. During the afternoon she usually spent an hour in meditation. At a certain time they closed the curtains around her bed and they would leave her alone...with the Queen of Heaven who came to visit her. After this she continued to work until 10:00 or 11:00 p.m. Then Luisa would write when she received some manifestation or communication from our Lord whether it happened during the day or while sleeping at night or at the time she received an order to write. Finally, now around 12:00 midnight or 1:00 a.m. Luisa laid down in her bed and entered her state of "death" and then lost the use of her senses. And if this happened before she could stretch out in bed, she would remain in that posture as though she were a statue of rock. And this is how the days of her life passed.

Now let us talk about Annibale Maria di Francia who, although he knew her for more than seventeen years, was only her special Confessor for less than two years and was in contact with her until his death in 1927. He became so interested in Luisa's life, her writings and the doctrine of the Divine Will that he published the "Hours of the Passion." Annibale Maria di Francia arrived at Corato in 1910. He began a series of visits and a special spiritual relation with Luisa. Meeting Luisa caused a transcendental change in his life. His knowledge about the Divine Will was the fundamental basis of his spirituality. The Archbishop of Trani appointed him as Ecclesiastical

Censor of the diocese to direct the publications related to Luisa's writings.

Fr. Di Francia dedicated all his energy to the publication of the "Hours of the Passion" for which he wrote a lengthy introduction. He published four editions, all of which had Imprimaturs and Nihil Obstats. As the Ecclesiastical Censor he obtained imprimaturs for the first nineteen volumes of Luisa's writings.

Let us direct our attention to the testimony which Fr. Di Francia left regarding Luisa:

"...She wishes to live in isolation, hidden and unknown. Never would she have put into writing the personal and prolonged communication with adorable Jesus from her earliest years until now — and which will continue until who knows when — if our Lord, Himself, had not obliged her. This obligation arose at times directly from our Lord and at times through holy obedience imposed by her spiritual directors. She submitted to this obedience with great fortitude and generosity even though it caused her immense suffering. Her obedience was so absolute that if directed she would even refuse Paradise. And this constitutes one of the most important characteristics of a virtuous, true and proven spirit. For forty years she struggles internally to submit herself and be dominated by "Lady Obedience..."

"This solitary soul is a most pure virgin, belonging totally to God, an object of singular predilection of our Divine Redeemer, Jesus. It seems our Lord, who across the centuries increases the marvels of his Love, wishes to make an instrument of this virgin. It is she who He calls the least significant and least instructed on the earth. Moreover, it seems our Lord wishes to form a most fit instrument for a mission so sublime that it cannot be compared to any other, that is, for the triumph of the Divine Will on earth as it is stated in the 'Our Father': 'Fiat Voluntas tua, sicut in coelo et in terra' (May Your Will be done on earth as It is in Heaven.)

"Since she was an adolescent, this virgin of the Lord was kept in bed for more than forty years as a victim of Divine Love. During all this time she has experienced an extensive series of natural and supernatural sufferings while enraptured in the eternal Charity of the Heart of Jesus. The origin of the pain that exceeded all boundaries was the prolonged, intermittent deprivation of Jesus..."

"Sufferings of the soul were added to those of the body. All these sufferings originated from her mystical state without any manifestations on her hands, feet, side, or forehead. She received from out Lord Himself frequent crucifixion. And if Jesus did not make her suffer in this way, it would be an immensely greater spiritual suffering. And this is another sign of a genuinely virtuous soul..."

"Having elaborated at length about Luisa's long and continuous life of many years in bed as a victim soul and her participation in so much spiritual and physical pain, it would seem that the sight of such an unknown virgin would be painful and disturbing. It would be like watching someone bedridden with the signs of suffering. But here is another quality in that during the day when this Spouse of the Crucified Jesus was sitting in bed and doing her embroidering there was never the slightest clue to suggest she spent her nights in extreme suffering with every conceivable pain. But never was there any pretense of anything extraordinary or supernatural. She has, then, the aspect of a healthy, joyful and happy person. She talks, ponders and sometimes laughs with the few friends she receives..."

"Let me make one final point. The life of this virgin spouse of Jesus is more heavenly than earthly. She wishes to pass through this world unknown and ignored, searching for no one except Jesus and his Blessed Mother who has taken her under her special protection..."

And we say that this testimony is valid because Fr. Di Francia, knowing Luisa so well and for so many years and publishing the "Hours of the Passion" with such fervor, was beatified by Pope John Paul II on October 7, 1990. Fr. Di Francia was eulogized and was set forth as an example for the Priests of our time.

Luisa's Writings

We could relate innumerable, astonishing and extraordinary anecdotes about Luisa's life as do many who knew her. But to narrate such anecdotes runs the risk of reducing her life to a series of pious, edifying and miraculous episodes. It runs the risk of leaving behind what is most important about Luisa and what distinguishes her from all others — her mission.

Who, then, was Luisa? What did she accomplish in life? What was her mission? The answers to these questions are amazing. They are found in her very writings. It is impossible to know Luisa apart from her writings. Her writings not only inform us about her interior life, but enable us to arrive at the knowledge of the formation of her life in us: **The Life Of The Divine Will.**

But before being astonished by her writings, we wish to present two testimonies given by aforementioned Priests, Fr. Domenico Franze and Fr. Consalvo Valls. They are the following:

Dear Father,

Almost a year ago last September, your Excellency, along with another dignitary, interviewed me regarding two manuscripts of the book entitled "In the Reign of the Divine Will." It was your wish that I render a judgment about the book whose author had sought absolute anonymity. Well, Reverend Father, as you know, I wasn't content in just reading the book but wanted to also meet the author so as to better be able to render an opinion.

Having read the book and met the author, I didn't stop with my own convictions, but sought the opinions of some competent religious colleagues. I am enclosing one such testimony. It is the opinion of Fr. Consalvo Valls, professor of Theology in our university, the International University of St. Anthony. He is currently in charge of revising our text books. I will include his testimony later.

Truthfully, anyone not having time nor interest in examining the book can simply review the index to see how this soul, called by God to perfection, is gradually elevated through self-annihilation, anonymity and detachment, through temptations and trials, one of which is most severe and has lasted more than 46 years.

I am simply astounded as a medical doctor to find no bed sores or skin abrasions on a patient who has been obliged to be immobile in bed for so many years.

As a Religious Examiner, it is most consoling to have received assurances that for many years and after exhaustive examinations by physicians, Confessors and Archbishops, no one has ever discovered any deception.

And finally, as a Priest I am delighted to have confirmed that in this patient there exists not only a refined integrity of Christian virtue but a movement of a soul striving toward a perfection illuminated by a special grace.

Aside from all that it seems our Lord deigned to accomplish in this soul to purify and make her a worthy instrument of mercy for others, I observe in her writings the prevailing theme which I would call the paramount meaning of the existence of this creature: **The Divine Will.**

This humble soul calls upon everyone to comprehend the evil of their personal wills and proclaims that just as the human will represents a common evil which is sin, so also there exists for sinful mankind a universal remedy. This remedy is that the **Most Holy Will Of God Be The Life Of The Human Will.**

If this book did nothing more than impress on its readers the rights of God and his Most Holy Will and affirm his supreme power over the human will and over the power and kingdoms of our minuscule earth, I would still maintain that it would make a significant contribution for the good of souls.

Reverend Father, I tell you that it is my judgment both as a Priest and physician that only a mortified and continuously mortified soul, **Only A Human Will Fused In The Divine Will** could arrive at concepts so basic and fundamental as those which this soul reveals. And this is achieved without studies or schooling, being only on a bed of pain and spasm, with an extremely limited background in literature, theology or asceticism. Yet she **Speaks With True Competence** about the most obscure themes and gives solutions to the most difficult problems and **Takes The Soul Of Who Reads Her Writings To The Most Aromatic Spheres Of Virtue.**

It is not the time, however, for me to explain the physical, psychophysical and moral proofs which I have found in this patient. I have moral certitude and, having 65 years of good experience and divorced from worldly concerns and excesses, I reaffirm this moral certitude in as far as it is given to man that the book which your Excellency gave me can achieve a great good, above all because it comes from an unpretentious and virtuous soul.

I thank you for the memorable occasion you have given me and I commend myself to your prayers.

Most respectfully yours in Christ,

Fray Domenico Franze, Medical Surgeon

Professor of Physiology and Missionary Medicine,
International University of St. Anthony
Honorary member of the Pontifical Roman Academy
of Missions in Rome

July 20, 1931

Regarding Fr. Valls' testimony which Fr. Franze mentions, we transcribe only the main points which are the following:

"Reverend Fr. Franze:

I have read and studied the book entitled "In the Reign of the Divine Will" and, having meditated on some of the themes, I am able to state the following:

I. Relative to Dogma: I find it to completely conform with the teachings of the Holy Church and those revealed in the sources of Revelation, including when it speaks in a passing manner on questions of dogma as... (and then follows a series of analyses and commentaries such as: "sublime and marvelous theological precision...", "also the concept is most precise... without dissonance and with marvelous harmony." "Concepts are never repeated yet new and most beautiful aspects are presented without ever for an instant deviating from the truths of the Faith", etc.). It is true that on occasion incertitudes are encountered, including, at times, unusual things which need explanation. But it is also true that when one reflects more on these thoughts, the dissonance of the first impression disappears. Moreover, Jesus, Himself, gives assurances when He calms her fears of writing nonsense.

II. Relative to asceticism: The book is most exact with respect to the judgments that are presented, especially when treating the active means of sanctification (prayer, work, fulfilling responsibilities, sacraments, pious practices, mortification, etc.) and the virtues.... (Note: to justify all the author's points, one would need to quote the entire book...).

III. With respect to mystical phenomena: The book seems to be truly inspired. (Of the numerous points that are presented, we mention one as an example: "the difference between the abstract and intuitive knowledge of God and of the soul itself. The intuitive explanation is one that is both psychological and experimental. It explains the theological doctrine regarding the Divine Gifts of the Holy Spirit acting in man and how these Divine Acts differ in nature from the human acts which man accomplishes using his own virtue.

IV. With respect to the self-portrait of this soul: It is evident that she intensely lives the life of Grace from which she creates the most beautiful and exact descriptions. And only the gifts of the Holy Spirit could give her the knowledge and, still more, the science to describe them. This contemplation of God in his attributes and Trinitarian Life comes from the full use of these gifts. The same can be said of her contemplation of Christ and the Most Holy Virgin in their mysteries and this vision — so consoling and marvelous — of the Divine Will which governs the world. Such resolution and generosity can come from no other source other than Divine Grace which absorbs the being of this soul. With these virtues she undergoes the greatest and most profound sacrifices which our Lord requests of her. Her sensitive and acute sentiments, along with her immense charity toward others springs from and has its foundation in the love of Jesus. And, moreover, **The Substitution Of One's Own Will For The Will Of Our Lord** can only come from Grace which allows her to remain peaceful, secure and content in the midst of the greatest tribulation, sufferings and aridity. And this constitutes the particular mission of this soul.

From all of these observations, made in passing, I harbor the conviction that the person in question is a soul of God and that the **Work Being Accomplished In Her Is Divine.** Although I do not know about the life or history of this soul, my examination of the book and the effect which I myself have experienced with her discourse permits me to take this position. This discourse has placed in my spirit a new yearning for a more intense spirituality. Only God holds the keys to man's heart and causes it to vibrate toward sanctification..."

With deepest regard to your Reverence,

Fray Consalvo Valls, O.F.M.
Professor of Dogmatic and Mystical Theology
International University of St. Anthony, Rome

What is it, then, about Luisa that distinguishes her from all the others? Quickly said and with simple words: she was the first to live in the Divine Will with perfect imitation of the Humanity of our Lord: "My food is to do the Will of my Father" ...and the perfect imitation of the most Holy Virgin: "Let it be done to Me..."

The Saints and the Church have known until now the conformity with the Will of God, the complete abandonment, even the **Union** with God's Will, with his Divine Volition. We can see examples of this from such Saints as St. Francis de Sales or St. Vincent de Paul (and, for that matter, hundreds of other Saints) in the expression: "to empty oneself of himself and unite his will totally to God's such that there is only one will with his." We could say that this is the highest point. And how does Luisa's doctrine differ from this union of wills? Let us take the answer from her writings. In the chapter dated Oct. 6, 1922 (Vol. 14), Luisa asks the question how it is that she was the first to **Live In The Divine Will** after so many centuries and so many Saints in the church. Our Lord responds: ...moreover, it is certain that I have called you first over other souls. Because to no other souls, however much I have loved them, have I shown **How To Live In My Will, The Effects, The Marvels, The Riches That The Creature Receives Who Acts In My Supreme Will.** Search the lives of the Saints as much as you wish or in books of doctrine and you will not find the wonders of **My Will Working In The Creature And The Creature Acting In My Will. The Most You Will Find Will Be Resignation, Abandonment, The Union Of Wills, But The Divine Will Working In The Creature And The Creature In My Will, You Will Not Find This In Anyone.** This signifies that the time had not arrived in which my kindness would call the creature to live in such a sublime state. Moreover, even the way I ask you to pray is not found in any other..."

This is to say that from the union of wills, which has been already experienced, Luisa enters into the unity of **Wills** and into the **Activity** of that **Unity**, to the **Activity And Life** of the creature in the **Divine Will,** along with Its effects, etc.

The reader will be able to completely corroborate this assertion if he reads these writings without prejudice and with a mind open to the light of the Truth." If they are not read in this manner, the reader "will not understand anything" (Vol. 12, Jan. 18, 1919).

The first selections will be taken from different volumes which do not, consequently, provide a continuous theme through the chapter dated September 18, 1938. From that point, the chapters are all presented more sequentially, providing a growing pedagogy, taking the reader progressively to greater truths and understanding. It is, therefore, recommended that these chapters be read in order, at least for the first time they are read. The titles preceding the chapters were not written by Luisa, but are presented only to aid in identifying their content.

José Luis Acuña R.

*   *   *

*The following texts are selected
from the*

Book of Heaven,

written by the Servant of God,

Luisa Piccarreta

January 29, 1919

"My beloved daughter, I want you to know the order of my Providence. In every 2000-year period I have renewed the world. In the first period I renewed it with the Flood. In the second 2000 years, I renewed it with my coming to the earth and manifesting my Humanity from which, as so many channels of light, my Divinity shone. And in this third period of 2000 years, those who are good and the Saints themselves **Have Lived The Fruits Of My Humanity**, but have enjoyed my Divinity scarcely at all.

"Now we are at the end of the third period and **There Will Be A Third Renovation.** This is why there is general confusion. It is due to the preparation for the third renovation. And if in the second renovation I manifested what **My Humanity Did And Suffered, Little Was Said About The Working Of My Divinity.** Now in this third renovation, after the purging of the earth and the destruction of a large part of the present generation, I will be still more generous with creatures. **I Will Complete The Renovation By Manifesting What My Divinity Did In My Humanity**, how my Divine Will **Worked With My Human Will,** how everything remained joined in Me, how I did and redid everything, and even the thoughts of each creature were redone by Me and sealed with my Divine Will. **My Love Wishes To Release Itself And Make Known The Excesses That My Divinity Worked In My Humanity** for creatures. These excesses greatly surpass those which my Humanity visibly worked. This is why I often speak to you about **Living In My Will Which I Have Not Manifested To Anyone Until Now.** At most they have known the shadow of my Will, the grace, enchantment and sweetness which It contains. **But To Penetrate Within,** to embrace Its immensity, to multiply one's self with Me, to penetrate everywhere, even while on earth, to penetrate into heaven and into hearts, to abandon human ways

1

And Work With Divine Ways... This is not yet known. And this is so true that it will appear strange to many, and whoever does not have his mind open to the light of the truth will understand nothing. But, little by little, I will make my way, manifesting at different times truths about my Will in such manner that they will finally understand."

July 16, 1922

And Jesus, in perfect kindness, said to me: "My daughter, take courage and don't be discouraged. I will also be with you in this. Your will must disappear before Mine. Besides, it is the Sanctity of my Will that wishes to be known; this is the reason. The Sanctity of living in my Will does not have a pathway, nor keys, nor rooms. It encompasses everything. It is like the air that one breathes, air that all can and should breathe. All that is necessary is that they want it and that they put aside their human will. Then the Divine Will will breathe through their soul. It will give the soul the life, the effects, and the value of Life in my Will. **But If It Is Not Known, How Will They Be Able To Love And To Want Such A Holy Life.** It is the greatest glory that the creature can give Me.

"The sanctity of the other virtues is quite known throughout the Church and whoever wants can imitate it. For that reason I am in no hurry to disseminate its knowledge. **But The Sanctity Of Living In My Will, Its Effects, The Worth That It Contains, The Final Touch That My Creative Hand Will Give The Creature To Make Him Similar To Me Is Not Yet Known. This Is Why It Is Urgent That All I Have Said To You Be Known.** And if you do not do this, you would, so to speak, restrict my Will and repress in Me the flames that consume Me and cause Me to delay the complete glory that Creation owes Me. But I want things to go forth in order, because

2

one word that is lacking, a comma, an insight that is lacking, a chapter half finished, instead of illuminating, it will cast forth shadows; and, instead of giving Me glory and love, creatures will remain indifferent... Be attentive, therefore, because I want nothing of what I have said to be lost."

And I: "But in order to present everything of yours, I am obliged to put something of my own." And Jesus: "And, what are you saying with this? If we have walked this path together, do you want Me to go alone? Besides, who should be pointed out and set as an example to follow, if the one I have schooled and who practices living in my Will does not want to be known? My daughter, this is absurd." ...

February 10, 1924

"...in my All-Seeingness I see that **These Writings Will Be For My Church As A New Sun** that will rise in her midst. And men, attracted by its radiant light, will strive to transform themselves into this light to become spiritualized and divinized, thereby, **Renewing The Church, They Shall Transform The Face Of The Earth.**

"The doctrine on my Will is the most pure, the most beautiful, not subject to any shadow of what is material or of self-interest, both in the supernatural as well as the natural order. Therefore, it will be as the sun which is the most fecund and the most welcomed. And since it is Light, by itself it will make its own way and make itself understood. It will not be subject to doubts or suspicion of error. And if some word is not understood, it will be because the excessive Light eclipses man's intelligence which is unable to grasp the fullness of the Truth. But man will not find a single word that is not the Truth. At most, he will be unable to completely understand it.

"Therefore, in view of the good that I see, I urge you to omit nothing in writing. A saying, an effect, a simile about my Will can be as a beneficent dew upon souls, as the dew upon the plants is beneficent after a day of scorching sun or as a downpour after long months of drought. You cannot understand all the good, the light and the force there is within a single word. But your Jesus knows and He knows who it will benefit and the good that it must do."

Now, while He said this, He showed me a table in the midst of the Church with all the Divine Will writings placed on it. Many venerable persons surrounded the table; and they became transformed into Light and divinized, and as they walked they communicated this Light to whomever they encountered. And Jesus added: **"You Will See This Great Good From Heaven. The Church Will Receive This Heavenly Nourishment And, Having Been Strengthened, She Will Arise In Full Triumph."**

September 22, 1924

I continue: While I was writing what was said before, I saw my sweet Jesus who placed his mouth upon my heart. His breath inspired me with the words I was writing. And in those same moments I heard a horrible commotion at a distance, as though people were fighting and beating each other. They howled with such a noise that it was frightening.

Then, directing myself to my Jesus I said to Him: "My Jesus, my Love, who are they who are making such a commotion? They seem like furious demons. What do they want that they are fighting each other so much?"

And Jesus: "My daughter, indeed they are demons. They do not want you to write about my Will because when they see you write the most important truths **About Living In My Will,** they suffer double hell which torments the dammed even more. **They Are So Afraid That These Writings Will Be Published About My Will And That Their Kingdom On The Earth Will Be Lost.** This is the kingdom acquired by them when man, withdrawing from my Divine Will, gave free reign to his human will. Oh yes, it was precisely then that the enemy acquired his reign on the earth. **But In The Presence Of My Will, The Enemy Will Imprison Himself In The Deepest Abysses!** This is why they fight with such fury. They feel the Power of my Will in these writings and, due to the possibility they could be published, they become furious and try with all their power to hinder such a great blessing. But don't pay any attention to them; and because of this, learn to appreciate more my teachings..."

November 7, 1937

My poor mind felt overcome by so many truths that my sweet Jesus had me write concerning the Divine Will. I thought to myself: who knows when these written truths will come to light about the Divine Will and what will be the benefit? And my beloved Jesus, surprising me with his brief visit, with all kindness and tenderness said to me:

"My daughter, out of love I also feel you should know the sequence of events of these truths and the good they will do. These truths about my Divine Will will form the **Day Of My Fiat In The Midst Of The Creatures.** To the extent they become known, they will form that day. Accordingly, as you start to know the first truths I have revealed, **Given Your Good Will And Disposition To Make Them Your Own Life,** they will

5

form a splendid dawn. These truths will also have the power to dispose and give birth to so many who are blind and do not know or love my truths. Then, as the day breaks forth, they will feel invested with a heavenly peace, more reaffirmed in goodness. They will, as a consequence, long to know other truths which will form the beginning of the day of my Will. This beginning of the day will augment the light and the love. All things will be converted into good for them; passions will lose their power to lead them to sin. It can be said that this is the first order of divine good that they will feel. This order will facilitate their actions. They will feel the power of being able to do everything because it is precisely this fundamental quality that is put in the soul: to transform all her nature into good. Then, feeling the great good of the beginning of the day of my Will, they will long for the day to advance. And they will come to know other truths which will form the full day. In this full day they will feel **The Life Of My Will Alive In Them**, Its joys and happiness and Its operative and creative power. They will feel in possession of my same Life.... The morning will give them such longings to know the remaining truths which, when they become known, will form the full midday.

"Living in this reality, the creature will no longer feel alone. There will be no separation between him and my Will. What my Will does the creature will do. It will be acting with Me. By right everything will be his: Heaven and earth and even God Himself. Do you see, then, what a noble, divine and precious purpose these truths will serve that I have had you write concerning my Divine Will — to form Its day?! To some it will form the dawn, to others the beginning of the day, for others the morning, and lastly, for others the full midday. These truths, **In As Much As They Are Known**, will form the different stages of the souls who will live in my Will. One knowledge of more or of less will cause them to advance or remain in different levels. Knowledge will be the hand to assist them in advancing to superior levels. Knowledge will be the **Same Life Of The Fullness Of My Will In Them.** I can say, therefore, that with these truths I have formed the day for whomever wants to live in my Divine Will. It is the day of Heaven, more than Creation itself. Not a creation of sun and stars because each truth has the power to create our LIFE in the creature and, oh, how it surpasses every truth of Creation.

"Therefore, our Love has overcome everything in revealing so many truths about my Divine Will. Our Glory will be complete in man because he will have **Our Life In His Power To Glorify Us And Love Us...** Regarding how these truths come forth: just as I have had power and love to assist the one who should manifest them, so will I have the power and loveto invest the others and transform them into the same truths. And experiencing this life within them, they will feel the need to make them known. Then, don't worry. I, who can do all things, will do and take care of everything."

June 20, 1938

After this I was thinking about these blessed writings and because of the insistence of my beloved Jesus, I willingly continued writing... and I was thinking: "and after so many sacrifices, in whose hands will these writings end up?" And my beloved Jesus, interrupting my thought, said to me:

"My child, don't worry. I will be an attentive watchman because these writings have cost Me so much. They have cost Me my Will which enters these writings as Primary Life. I could call them an inheritance, **An Inheritance Of Love That My Will Gives To The Creature.** My Will becomes the Giver of Itself and calls the creature to live with his inheritance. It is done with such supplication, so appealing, so loving that only hearts of stone would not be moved to compassion and would not feel the necessity of receiving such a great benefit. These writings are full of divine lives which cannot be destroyed. And if someone would want to attempt it, it would happen to him as someone who would attempt to destroy the sky which, when offended, would fall on him and everywhere and would destroy him under its blue firmament... Much is needed to communicate what I have had you write about my Will. So I can call it a new Creation, a living and speaking Creation. This will be the last overflow of Love toward the human generations. You should know, moreover, that for each word I make you write about my FIAT, I duplicate my Love toward you and toward those who will read them so they will remain perfumed by my Love.

"Therefore, to the extent you write, you give Me the occasion to love you more. **I See The Great Good That These Writings Will Do.** I feel in each word the palpitating lives of the creature who will know the benefits of my words and will form the Life of my Will in them. Therefore, the interest will be all Mine; abandon everything to Me. You must know that these writings have come from the center of the great Sun of my Will whose rays are full of the truths emanating from this center. These are the truths that embrace all times, all centuries and all generations.... This great radiance of so much light fills Heaven and earth; and as light, it knocks at the doors of all hearts, and begs and pleads **That They Receive The Palpitating Life Of My Fiat,** which our Paternal Goodness has so benignly deigned to dictate [these writings] from within Its center with the most gracious, attractive, affable ways, full of sweetness and with a Love so great that it reaches to the incredible, so much so that it leaves the very Angels stupefied. Each word can be called a marvel of love, one greater than the other. Accordingly, wanting to touch these writings is to want to touch Me, the center of my Love, my loving kindness with which I love creatures....

And I will know how to defend Myself and how to confuse whoever might want to disclaim — in the least way — even one single word of all that is written about my Divine Will. Keep listening, then, to Me, my daughter, and don't hinder my Love nor tie my arms with the intention of repressing in my Bosom what you must continue writing. **These Writings Cost Me Greatly. They Cost Me As Much As I Myself Cost.** Because of this, I will take great care that not even one word will be lost."

May 14, 1935

My mind always returns to the immense ocean of the Divine Will which, while It whispers, smiles with love at his creature and, in exchange, urges him to reciprocate with tender smiles. And Its does not allow him to lag behind in demonstrating love; moreover, it becomes almost impossible for the creature not to do what the Divine Will does while he lives in It. Who can tell what the soul feels in this divine sea? She feels the purity of Its kisses; she enjoys all the joy of Its embraces which infuse her with heavenly peace, Divine Life, and such strength so as even to conquer God Himself. Oh, how much I would like that all men live in this sea... they would never leave it! And while I was thinking in this way, I said to myself: "But when will this Kingdom of the Divine Will come? Who will be able to see It? Oh, how difficult it seems for It to come!" Then Jesus, repeating his visit to my poor soul, said to me:

"My daughter, the Kingdom of the Divine Will will arrive without fail. You calculate in a human way and, therefore, Its advent seems difficult to you. The Supreme Being, on the other hand, uses his own divine measurements which are such that they attain in a very simple way what seems impossible to human intelligence. And besides, is it not the Queen of Heaven with her sweet reign who implores continually for this Kingdom to come to the earth? And when have We denied anything to this Heavenly Mother? Our Being is incapable of resisting the power of her supplication since the power She possesses is the very same that animates our Will. It is with the power of this force that She entreats with full right this Holy Kingdom which, without any doubt, will be granted Her; and, therefore, it also will be called the **'Kingdom Of The Heavenly Queen.'** And what will the Heavenly Mother and Queen not do for the people and her children who live in the Divine Will? She will bestow **Graces Never Heard Of**, surprises never known. She will work miracles that will move Heaven and earth. She will place at their disposition her own seas of grace, holiness and power and will put to flight all their enemies.

"And to keep them safe, She will surround them with her virtues, with her sufferings and with those of her Divine Son. She will let them grow up upon her own lap. She will hide them in her love; She will cover them with her light. By means of her own hands She will nourish them with the food of the Divine Will. How much work will these souls give Her and what joys She will experience when She transforms them into faithful copies of Herself by means of her most affectionate care and her most laborious and diligent, maternal tenderness! They will be her youngest children, her secretaries, the powerful magnets of those who will never be able to be separated from her gaze and **With Whom All Will Be Had In Common: Love And Life, Joys And Pain....** Living in my Will, they will form her sweetest company; they will participate in her maternal fecundity and **They Will Enjoy The Heritage Of Each Of Her Acts.**

"Oh, how happy and greatly rewarded this sweet Mother will feel when She sees that there is someone who understands Her, who resembles Her, who caresses Her, **Who Lives In God's Will Like Her.**"

10

December 8, 1936

"...until now, even the Holy Church has known only some of the features concerning the Holiness, greatness and gifts with which my Divine Mother was adorned. Only I can tell the true story of her life and reveal the marvels that were accomplished in Her by our Divine FIAT... "

"...Oh, how many divine secrets will be known by men when they understand what it means to **Live In My Will.**"

July 11, 1923

I was praying and completely abandoning myself in the arms of my sweetest Jesus, but a thought in my mind said to me: "This martyrdom of having to bother others is only for me. It is troublesome to be a burden to the ministers, not being able to do anything but bother them with the events taking place between Jesus and me. Others, on the other hand, are free. They enter a state of suffering and are able to free themselves. But I, how many times have I asked Him to free me, but in vain!"

Then, while I was thinking this and other things, Blessed Jesus came, all kindness and love, and placing Himself next to me, said: "My daughter, as big as the work is that I want to do, so much more is it necessary that the creature I choose be unique and singular. The work of Redemption was the greatest, and I chose a single creature. I bestowed on Her all gifts— never given to any creature — causing Her to contain so much grace to be my Mother and to deposit in Her all the benefits of Redemption. And, in order to watch over my own gifts from her Conception until my own, I held Her under the Light of the Holy Trinity, which became caretaker and held the office of directing Her in everything. Later, when I was conceived in her virginal womb, I, being the true Head and the first Priest, took the task of taking care of Her in everything, even in the movement of her pulse. And when I died, I entrusted Her to another Priest, Saint John. I did not want to leave a Soul so privileged, who contained all graces, unique in the Divine Mind and unique in history without the assistance of my representative until her last breath. Have I ever done this for other souls? No, because other souls did not contain so much good, so many gifts and so many graces. So much care and assistance, therefore, was unnecessary.

"Now, my daughter, you also are unique in my Mind; and you will be unique in history. There will not be — either before or after you — any other creature for whom I will obligate through necessity the assistance of my Ministers. It was convenient and proper that one of my Ministers attend you because you were chosen as a depository of **The Sanctity, The Good, The Effects And The Act Of My Supreme Will.** It was proper that my minister be the first keeper of the goods that my Will contains and from his bosom have them pass to all the body of the Church. How much attention is required from you and them. You, in receiving from Me, as a second mother, **The Great Gift Of My Will** and to know all Its qualities, and my ministers in receiving It from you **To Fulfill In My Church The 'Fiat Voluntas Tua'** in Heaven as It is on earth. Oh, you don't know how much I have had to give you to become the depository of my Will. I have taken from you all sources of corruption. I have purified your soul and your very nature so that you neither feel anything for them nor they for you. Because lacking the seeds of corruption is as if fire were lacking to firewood. And if I did not free you from Original Sin, as I did my dear Mother, by removing that source of corruption from you, I put into operation another prodigy of grace never bestowed on anyone else. Because it was proper for my Will, three times Holy, to descend and take possession of a soul without her

12

having been even minimally darkened by the slightest corrupt breath, my Will would not have adapted Itself to take possession of you and to communicate to you Its Act if I had seen in you any seeds of corruption. And I would not have adapted myself, Word of the Father, to be conceived in the womb of my Heavenly Mother if I had not freed her from Original Sin. And, moreover, how many graces have I not given you? You think it is nothing and, therefore, you don't even think of it. And instead of being grateful to Me you are busy thinking about what I have prepared for you and those who surround you while I only want you to continue in my Will.

"You should know that this fulfillment of my Will is so momentous that it enters into the greatest works that the Trinity has done. And I want It to be known so that, knowing the greatness and the immense benefits that It contains, souls will honor and desire It.

"Three times the Divinity decided to work 'ad extra' [outside Themselves]: the first was in Creation, and this was without the intervention of the creature. The second was in Redemption, and together with it a woman intervened, the holiest, the most beautiful, which was my Heavenly Mother. She was the channel and the instrument through which I accomplished the work of Redemption. **And The Third Is The Fulfillment Of My Will, Which Will Be Done On Earth As In Heaven, That Is, That Creature Might Live And Work With The Holiness And Power Of Our Will.** The work of Creation and Redemption are inseparable, just as the Sacrosanct Trinity is inseparable. We cannot say that We have finished the work of Creation if our Will, as it was decreed by Us, **Does Not Act In The Creature And Live With The Same Freedom, Holiness, And Power That Lives In Us.** Moreover, this is the most beautiful, brightest and supreme moment. It is the seal of fulfillment of the Work of Creation and Redemption. These are Divine

Decrees and must have their complete fulfillment. And in order to accomplish this decree, We want to utilize another woman, who is you. It was the woman who initiated the cause for man to cast himself headlong into his misfortunes. And We want to utilize a woman to restore order again and enable man to leave his misfortunes and restore to him respect, honor and our true likeness, as We created him.

"Therefore, be attentive. Don't take things lightly. It is no small matter; it is a matter of divine decrees, and it gives Us the occasion to complete the Works of Creation and Redemption. We entrusted my Mother to Saint John to deposit in him — and from him to the Church — the treasures, the graces and all my teachings during the course of my Life. Since my Mother was entrusted to Me and, being a Priest to Her, I entrusted to Her as a sanctuary all the laws, precepts and doctrines that the Church needed to possess. And, faithful as She was and zealous for even one of my words so they would not be lost, She deposited them in my faithful disciple, John. And for that reason my Mother has supremacy over all the Church. In the same way I have done this with you. Being necessary to serve the **Fiat Voluntas Tua** to all the Church, I have entrusted you to one of my ministers so that you might deposit in him everything I reveal to you about my Will: **The Goods That It Contains And How The Creature Should Enter Into It And How The Paternal Kindness Wants To Open Another Era Of Grace, Putting The Goods He Possesses In Heaven In Common With The Creature And Restoring To Man His Lost Happiness.** Because of this, be attentive and faithful."

August 14, 1926

My poor heart swims in a sea of bitterness for want of my sweet Jesus, who, if He comes, does so as a fleeting flash of lightning. In that flash I see the poor world, its grave ills, nations conniving among themselves to produce wars and revolution. And this brings down chastisements from Heaven which will destroy entire cities and towns. Oh God! How great is humanity's blindness!

After this fleeting flash of his lovable presence, I remain in greater darkness than before, alone with the thought of my poor brothers and sisters scattered in this hard life of exile. But as if this were not enough to fill my heart with intense bitterness, another source of bitterness was added, almost enough to drown out my poor existence: the news that the writings on the Most Holy Will of God, with the approval and imprimatur of our Archbishop, would soon be published. But the most severe blow to my poor soul has been the news that it was not just the writings about the Divine Will that were to be published. I had become reconciled to the publication of such writings by the insistence of Our Lord and my superiors, who had convinced me that this was for the Glory of God. Thus it was not for me, small and miserable as I am, to oppose the desires of Blessed Jesus. What worries me now is that even the succession of interactions that Jesus has had with me and everything He has told me, even concerning the virtues and other diverse issues will also be published... and this has caused me much pain. I have stated and repeated many times my reasons for not wanting this done.

While I found myself so distraught, my sweet Jesus moved within me as if He, too, felt the weight of my oppression. Embracing me in his arms, He said by way of encouragement: "My daughter, what is it? What is it? Don't be downcast! I don't want you to be depressed. Instead of thanking Me you become depressed! You must know that in order for my Supreme Will to be known, I have had to prepare the circumstances, make available the means and overwhelm the Bishop by the sheer force of my Will, which no man can resist. I have had to work one of my great prodigies. Do you think it is easy to obtain the approval of a Bishop? Oh! How much vacillation, how many difficulties! And then, when what I have revealed out of my goodness is approved, they approve it with so many restrictions, almost stripping it of its most beautiful traits, of its most resplendent colors. Don't you see in the approval of the Bishop the triumph of my Will and, consequently, my great glory? Don't you comprehend the enormous need for the knowledge of the Supreme Will to be propagated so that, as a beneficent dew it may quench the fires of passions and, as a sun which rises, illuminate the darkness of the human will to eradicate the lethargy which, for want of living in my Will, overcomes almost all creatures even when they do good?

"These revelations regarding my Volition will be as a balm to heal the wounds produced by the human will. Whoever has the benefit of this knowledge will feel the flow of a new life of light, of grace and of strength to fulfill my Will in everything. Moreover, comprehending the great evil of self-will, he will abhor and will throw off the oppressive yoke of the human will to place himself under the gentle dominion of my Will. Ah! You don't know nor can you see what I see and know. Therefore let Me act and don't be downcast. On the contrary, you should have encouraged him [Blessed Fr. Annibale Maria di Francia] whom I have selected with so much love to do this work.

"My daughter, the Kingdom of my Will is invincible. **In These Writings I Have Placed Superabundant Light, Grace And Attraction To Make My Kingdom Victorious. To The Extent That These Writings Become Known, They Will Wage A Sweet Battle Against The Human Will And Will Win. This Knowledge Will Be As A Wall — Most High And Strong — More Than In The Earthly Paradise [Garden Of Eden] Which Will Impede The Infernal Enemy From**

16

Coming In To Provoke Those Who, Conquered By My Volition, Will Enter Into Its Kingdom. Don't be disturbed, then, and let Me act. I will arrange everything so that the Supreme FIAT will be known."

September 13, 1926

After making my usual rounds in the Divine Will, I was asking my good Jesus, on behalf of his Creation and Redemption and all men from the first to the last, on behalf of the Sovereign Queen and all She did and suffered, that the Supreme FIAT be known so that his Kingdom would be established and enter into Its full triumph and dominion. And as I did this, I thought to myself: "If Jesus Himself wants so much that his Kingdom be established among creatures, then why does He want us to ask for It so insistently? If He wants, He can give It without so many continuous requests." Then my sweet Jesus, moving within me, said:

"My daughter, my Supreme Being Possesses perfect equilibrium and remains so when It gives creatures my gifts and graces, and more so in giving this Kingdom of my Supreme Fiat, which is the greatest of Gifts and which I gave to man at the beginning of Creation and was so ungratefully rejected by him. Do you think it a small matter to place the Divine Will with all the goods It contains at the disposal of mankind, not just for one hour or one day but for life, or that the Creator deposit in a creature his adorable Will in order to share with the creature his likeness, his beauty, his oceans of wealth, of joy and endless happiness? Merely by possessing our Will a creature acquires the right of ownership-in-common, of likeness, and of all the goods of his Creator. Without our Supreme Fiat a creature has nothing in common with Us; and if he does manage to take something, it is as mere droplets, small crumbs, pennies from among our infinite riches. And then to have such a Gift rejected, a Gift so great, a happiness so immense, a right to Divine Likeness, acquiring the nobility of belonging to our family. Do you think it a simple matter for the Divine Sovereignty to give this Kingdom of the Divine FIAT to creatures without It being requested or anyone giving the slightest thought to It or having the slightest desire to receive It? It would be a repetition of the history of the earthly Paradise... and perhaps worse! Furthermore, our Justice would be justly opposed to this.

"This is the reason for everything I ask you to do, all your continuous rounds in the Supreme Will, your unceasing prayers calling for my Will to come and reign, your life of sacrifice over so many years during which you know neither Heaven nor earth, a life dedicated to the sole end of calling down my Kingdom... these are like repeated supports before my Justice to surrender its rights. Justice, then, in balance with all our other attributes, finds it just that the Kingdom of the Supreme FIAT with all the good It contains be restored to human generations.

"The same thing occurred in the Redemption. If our Justice had not found the prayers, the sighs, the tears, the penances of the Patriarchs, Prophets and all the good people of the Old Testament and, moreover, a Virgin Queen who possessed our Will integrally and who took everything upon Herself with so many unceasing prayers, taking upon Herself the work of making satisfaction for all the human race, our Justice never would have conceded to the descent of the desired Redeemer among creatures. Our Justice would have been inexorable and would have given a resounding NO to my coming to earth. Because, my daughter, when it comes to maintaining the equilibrium of our Supreme Being it is not about doing nothing. Besides, who, until now, has ever requested with interest, with insistence, sacrificing his own life so that the Kingdom of the Supreme FIAT might come over the earth and that It triumph and establish Its

18

dominion? No one! It is true that ever since I came to the earth the Church prays the 'Our Father' which asks that my Kingdom come so that my Will be done on earth as It is in Heaven. But who thinks of what they are asking for? It can be said that all the importance of this request remained in my Will and that creatures pray it only to pray it, without really comprehending, nor having real interest in obtaining what they are asking for.

"Do you see now, my daughter, why it could not be given before? Since everything on this earth is cloaked in secret and seems a mystery and man can scarcely acquire but the slightest understanding of anything, man always has something to say about everything I reveal through my creatures. He even goes so far as to say 'Why hasn't this good, this knowledge, been given to us earlier if there have been such great Saints?' But in Eternity there are no secrets. I will reveal everything and will make all my just actions visible so that all will see that my Justice could never have given my Will to creatures if it had not found sufficient acts to justify giving what the Supreme Majesty was desirous of giving. It is true that everything that creatures do is by my grace, but the same grace wants to find the affirmation, disposition and good will of creatures.

"Therefore, to reestablish the Kingdom of my Will on earth, there must be sufficient acts by creatures to keep my Kingdom from remaining suspended and enable It to descend and take form upon the very acts which creatures have formed in order to obtain such an immense good. This is why I urge you so much to make your rounds in all our works, our Creation and Redemption. I do it to have you contribute your acts, your 'I love You', your adoration, your recognition and your 'thank You' over all our works. Many times I have made these rounds with you; and, as you finish your journey in our Will, you repeated, to honor Us, your refrain which is so pleasing to Us: *'Supreme Majesty, your little daughter comes before You; and I*

19

sit on your paternal knees, to request your FIAT, your Kingdom, that It may be known by all. I ask for the triumph of your Will so that It will establish Its dominion and reign in all. I am not alone in making this request. Together with me are all your works, your own Will. Therefore, on behalf of all, I request, I beg your FIAT.'

"Oh, if you only knew how powerfully your refrain impacts our Supreme Being. We feel Ourselves asking for all our works and begging for our own Volition. Heaven and earth kneel to petition the Kingdom of our Eternal Volition. Then, if, in truth, you want this Kingdom, continue with your acts so that when the established number has been completed, you can obtain that for which you sigh with such much insistence."

September 18, 1938

I am in the sea of the Divine Volition with immense bitterness and humiliation as one condemned. And if Jesus had not been my support, strength, and help, I don't know how I would have lived. Then my sweet Jesus, taking a portion of my pain, suffered with me. And in the flames of his Love and pain, He said:

"My dear daughter, if you knew how I suffered, if you could see it, you would die of pain. So as not to afflict you more, I am obligated to hide everything, all the intensity and severity of the pain I suffer. **You Must Know That They Have Not Condemned You, But Me With You**. I feel my sentence because to condemn what is good is to condemn Me Myself. In my Will unite your sentence with Mine, to what I suffered when crucified, **And I Will Give You The Merit Of My Sentence And All The Goods It Produced:** it brought about my death and brought to life my Resurrection in which all should find the life and resurrection of all goods. **With Their Sentence They Believe They Have Brought Death To What I Have Said About My Divine Will**, but I will permit such scourges and difficult times that **I Will Make My Truths** rise more beautifully and majestically in the midst of the towns. Therefore, on your part and Mine, let us continue in what we have done. It isn't important that everyone opposes us. This is my divine manner. It doesn't matter how many evil acts creatures do. I never leave my works but conserve them always with my Power and Creative Force for love of those who offend Me. I love them always without ever ceasing. Because We never stop, our works are completed and always remain beautiful, doing good to everyone. And if We would stop, each thing and everything would end in ruin; and no good would be completed. Therefore, I also want you with Me in this, always resolute, without ever leaving my Will doing what you have done until now, to attentively listen to Me, to be the narrator of my Will.

"**My Daughter, Whatever Is Not Enjoyed Today Will Be Enjoyed Tomorrow. What Appears Darkness Now, Because Of Minds That Are Blind, Will Change To Sunlight For Those Who Will Have Eyes To See. Oh, What Great Good They Will Do!** Let us, then, continue what we have done. Let us do what is necessary so that nothing is lacking, neither assistance nor light, nor good, nor surprising truths **So That My Volition Might Be Known And Reign.** I will use all the means of Love, of grace, of chastisements. I will influence the creature in every way to make my Volition reign; **And When It Seems As Though The True Good Should Die, It Will Rise More Beautiful And Majestic.** Therefore, take courage, my daughter; do not despair; trust in Me... I will think of everything and will defend the rights of my Volition **To Make It Reign.**

September 27, 1938

"Everything I have said regarding my Will I can explain by saying that It is a **New Creation,** more beautiful, more bountiful, more majestic than the very Creation everyone now sees! Oh how far this one falls behind! And as it is impossible for men to destroy or extinguish the light of the sun or stop the impetuous wind, or avoid the air they breathe or reduce everything to a pile of rubbish, much more so will they be unable to extinguish or destroy anything of what I have said. It is a new Creation which speaks, and each truth carries the mark and seal of our Divine Life. Therefore, in my manifested truths are included the suns which speak, the winds that talk and embrace in my Will so as to surround and conquer the creature with my Power. In these truths are my beautiful, varied creations which will enrapture each creature; seas of Love which will continuously inundate them and with their sweet murmurs will conquer hearts so that they will love Me. In these truths I have placed all possible and imaginable goods, love that conquers, enraptures, sweetens and moves the heart. Nothing is lacking in order to conquer the creature and allow my Will to descend with decorum and majesty, in union with the army of my truths and reign in their midst. **The Creature Will Not Be Permitted To Silence This New Creation. I Will Know Well How To Guard And Defend It.**

"Moreover, my daughter, this new Creation was not a work done in six days, but more than fifty years. So how could I permit that it be repressed or that it not have life or become known? **This Would Be The Same As Not Having Sufficient Power,** and this cannot be. I will guard it. They will not be able to destroy nor touch one word of Mine! It costs dearly, and when things cost much, all available resources, all skills are employed, even one's own life in order to attain the purpose. For this reason, allow Me to accomplish the work of this new

Creation. Don't worry about what they say or do...this is merely human caprice. With one breath of air they see black, and with another they take off their blindfolds and see white. **So I Will Know How To Overcome Everything And Make My Truths Known Like A Militant Army To Conquer The Creature.** Patience is needed, on my part as well as yours, so that We can continue forward without compromise."

*   *   *

[From this point onward the selected passages are in chronological order.]

February 12, 1906

The Virtues Let Us Arrive at a Certain Height. In the Divine Will There Are No Boundaries.

Finding myself in my usual state, I felt very oppressed because of the privation of my Blessed Jesus. Then He came and said to me: "My daughter, all the virtues of the creature build a wall of a different and determined height, but the wall of the soul that lives in the Divine Will is a wall so high and so deep that its limits cannot be known. It is a wall of pure, solid gold. It is not subject to any disaster because, being in the Divine Volition, that is to say, in God, He Himself takes care of her — and against God there is no power that can avail. By living in this Divine Volition, the soul is clothed in a light similar to the Light of the One in Whom she lives. And even in Heaven she will shine more brightly than the others and will be for the very Saints the cause of greater glory.

"Oh, my daughter, think a little about what an environment of peace and benefits is contained in only the words: 'Will of God!' The soul, with just the thought of wanting to live in this environment, already feels herself changed. A Divine

23

atmosphere clothes her; she feels herself lose her human essence and feels herself divinized. If she is impatient, she becomes patient; if she is proud, she becomes humble, docile, charitable and obedient. In summary, from being poor, she becomes rich; and all the virtues arise to encircle her with a wall so high that it has no limits. In this way the soul becomes lost in God, losing her own limits and acquiring those of the Divine Will."

July 3, 1906

How the Divine Will Is Paradise for the Soul and for God

Having received Holy Communion, I felt all united and very close to my most Divine Jesus; and while He hugged me, I rested in Him and He in me. Afterwards He said to me: "The soul who lives in my Will rests, because the Divine Will does everything for her; and I, while I am working for her, find there my most beautiful rest so that the Will of God is rest for the soul and rest for God in the soul. And the soul, while she rests in my Will, is always clinging to my mouth and receives the Divine Life, forming from It her continual food. The Will of God is the Paradise of the soul on earth, and the soul that does the Will of God comes to form the Paradise of God on the earth. The Will of God is the only key that opens the treasures of the Divine secrets. And the soul acquires such a familiarity in the House of God that she rules as though she were the owner."

Who can say all that I understood about this Divine Will? Oh, Will of God, how admirable, amiable, desirable and beautiful You are! It suffices to say that finding myself in You, I feel myself losing all my miseries and ills, acquiring a new essence with the fullness of all the Divine goods.

July 17, 1906

To Him Who Lives in the Divine Will, Jesus Gives the Keys of His Treasures

This morning I saw Blessed Jesus with some keys in his hand, and He said to me: "My daughter, this is the key to my Will. It is fitting that she who lives in my Will have the key to open and close as she pleases and thus be able to take what she likes of my treasures. Because, living in my Volition, she will care for these treasures more than if they were her own and will not waste them. Furthermore, she will give them to others and will take for herself what can give Me the most honor and glory. That is why I give you the key. Take care of my treasures." While He was saying this, I felt myself all submerged in the Divine Will and could not see anything else. I spent all day in this Paradise of his Will. What happiness! What joy!

Continuing in this ambience during the night, Jesus said to me: "My dear one, look at how for the one who lives in my Volition there is no grace that goes forth from my Will toward all the creatures in Heaven or on earth in which he is not the first to take part. This is natural because he who lives in the house of his father abounds in his possessions. And if those on the outside receive anything, it is in virtue of him who lives inside."

November 28, 1906

The Immense Good of Working in Close Union with Jesus

Continuing in my poor state, I saw my Blessed Jesus; and it seemed that He transformed Himself completely in me, such that if I breathed, I felt his breath in mine; if I moved an arm, I felt his move in mine; and it was this way for everything. And while He was doing this, He said to me: "My dear daughter, do you see in what close union of life I Am with you? This is how I want you, united closely to Me. But do not think that you should do this only when you pray or when you suffer; no, rather, always, always. If you move, if you breathe, if you work, if you eat, if you sleep, you should do everything as though you did it in my Humanity, as though all your acts came forth from Me.

So, then, nothing should be yours. Rather, everything should be in you only like a shell. And when this shell of your act is opened, inside should be found the fruit of the Divine Act. You should do everything in this way, on behalf of all the creatures, as if my Living Humanity were in the midst of all the creatures. Because by doing everything with the intention of receiving Life from Me, even the most indifferent and small actions acquire the merit of my Humanity.

I, being man and God, contained everything in Myself; that is to say, in my breath I contained the breaths of everyone; in my movement I contained the movements of everyone, in my thinking, the thoughts of everyone; and, therefore, I reformed and sanctified everything. Now you, acting in everything with the intention and attitude of receiving your acts from Me, you also come to embrace and contain all creatures in yourself; and your act will be diffused for the good of everyone. Then, in spite of the fact that all the others don't give Me anything, I shall take everything from you." Having said this, He disappeared.

I would have preferred to remain silent concerning all these things because, since they are intimate, I do not know how to manifest them clearly. But may all be for the Glory of God.

December 15, 1906

How the Divine Will Contains All Benefits

Continuing in my usual state, I was more bitter than ever because of the privation of my Jesus. Then, in an instant I felt as absorbed in the Will of God; and I felt such a calm come over all my interior that I did not feel myself anymore; rather, I felt everything in the Divine Volition, even the very privation of Jesus. Then I said to myself: "What strength, what enchantment, what attraction this Divine Will contains, even to making me forget myself... !" I was just saying this, when Jesus moved in my interior and said to me: "My daughter, since the Divine Will is the only substantial food, containing all the flavors and tastes that are fitting and appropriate for the soul, there she finds her exquisite food and becomes calm; the desire finds its food and thinks of nourishing itself; the inclinations have nowhere to be directed because they have what satisfies them. The will has nothing else to desire, and letting go of itself, which has caused its own torment, it finds the Divine Will, which forms all its happiness. It has left poverty and found riches, not those that are human, but those that are Divine.

"In summary, all the interior of the soul finds its food, that is to say, its activity in which it stays occupied and absorbed, not being able to go on to other things, because in this food and activity it finds all contentments. It finds so much to do and to learn; and, in always tasting new things, that the soul passes from a lesser knowledge to learn greater knowledge; and from small things she passes to great things; from one pleasing thing she passes on to other, superior enjoyments. And there is always something more to enjoy in this environment of the Divine Will."

January 20, 1907

The Greatest Sanctity to Which One Can Aspire Is to Live in the Divine Volition.

Having read the lives of two women Saints, one who had a great desire to suffer and the other who wanted to be little, I was thinking in my interior: "Which of the two sanctities is better, in order to be able to imitate it?" Not knowing how to resolve this, I felt rather oppressed.

Meanwhile, in order to be free from these thoughts and to think only about loving Jesus, I said to myself: "I do not want to aspire to anything except to love Him and fulfill perfectly his Holy Volition." I was just saying this when my Blessed Jesus said to me:

"And I want you here, in my Volition. Do you not know that unless the grain of wheat is buried under the earth and dies completely, it cannot come forth again to new life and multiply itself? Thus the soul, until she is buried in my Will and dies completely in It, by disintegrating her volition in Mine, cannot come forth again to a new Divine Life with the resurgence of all the virtues of Christ which contain the true Sanctity. For this reason, let my Will be the seal that marks all your interior and your exterior; and when everything has come forth again in you, there you will find true Love. That is the best of all the Sanctities to which the creature can aspire."

June 23, 1907

The Soul Who Abandons Herself in the Divine Will Reacquires God with All His Benefits.

Finding myself in my usual state, Blessed Jesus had not come; and I was thinking to myself: "What would be the most beautiful act and the most acceptable to Our Lord that might most induce Him to come: sorrow for one's sins or patient submission?" At this moment, Jesus came and said to me:

"My daughter, the most beautiful act that most pleases Me is abandonment in my Will, abandonment to the extent that one does not remember that his own essence exists, but only the Divine Volition. Although sorrow for one's faults is good and praiseworthy, it does not destroy one's own essence. On the other hand, abandoning oneself completely in my Will destroys one's own essence and causes one to reacquire the Divine Essence. Then the soul, by abandoning herself in Me, gives Me more honor because she gives Me all I could require of the creature. She lets Me reacquire in Myself what had gone forth from Me, and the soul reacquires the only thing she should reacquire: God. And in reacquiring God, she reacquires all the benefits that God Himself possesses. It is only when the soul is completely in the Will of God that she reacquires God. And if she leaves my Will, she reacquires her own essence, together with all the evils of her corrupt nature."

July 1, 1907

In the Divine Will, the Sins of the Past Are Forgotten.

I was reading about a Saint who was always thinking about her sins and was always asking God for pardon and sorrow for her sins, and I said to myself: "Lord, what a comparison between this Saint and myself! I never think about my sins; on the other hand, she was always thinking about hers. Obviously I am wrong..." At that instant I felt Jesus move in my interior, and with a light He said to me: "Foolish, foolish one! You don't want to understand... When has my will produced sins or imperfections? My Will is always Holy, and he who lives in It becomes holy. He enjoys, eats, and thinks about all that my Will contains; and even though in the past he may have committed sins, finding himself in Beauty, in Holiness, in the immensity of the benefits that my Will contains, he forgets the evil, the ugliness, and the sinfulness of his past and remembers only the present. If he should leave my Will, returning to his own essence, it is not surprising that he remember sins and miseries. Fix well in your mind that in my Will these thoughts of sins or of oneself cannot enter; and if the soul feels them, it means that she is not stable, nor is she fixed inside Me; rather, she keeps escaping outside."

The next day, finding myself in my usual state, I saw Him; and He said to me: "My daughter, the Truth, no matter how much it may be persecuted, cannot help but be recognized as being true. And sooner or later the time comes when that same persecuted Truth comes to be recognized and loved. In these sad times, all is falsehood and duplicity; and in order to make the Truth to rule, man merits being crushed and destroyed. Part of these chastisements they will give to themselves, and they will reciprocally destroy each other. Others will come from Me, especially for France, in which there will be such mortality that it will be left almost depopulated..."

July 4, 1907

The Soul Should Sow in Its Mind the Truths that Have Been Learned.

I was thinking about how I have been very bad, and nevertheless the Lord does not correct me or rebuke me. While I thought about this I felt Him move in my interior, and He said to me: "My daughter, keep going, keep going.... If I Am Goodness, Mercy, and Sweetness, I Am also Justice, Strength, and Power. Then, if I should see you regress or commit voluntary defects, in view of so many Graces that I have granted you, you would deserve to be struck down; and, indeed, I would do so. And if I don't, you yourself understand why. If I do not talk to you all the time, it is so that you sow in your mind the truths I have taught you. Then enter into your interior and unite yourself with Me, and I shall always be close to you to act interiorly with you."

July 19, 1907

In the Divine Will, Neither Aridities nor Defects Enter.

Having spoken with a person about the Will of God, I had told this person that being in the Will of God and feeling arid one could also be at peace.

Later, finding myself in my usual state, my Blessed Jesus corrected me, saying: "My daughter, pay close attention when you speak about my Will, because my Will is so happy that it forms Our very beatitude, and the human will is so unhappy that if it could enter into Ours, it would destroy Our happiness and would make war with Us. Therefore, in my Will neither aridities nor temptations nor defects nor agitations nor coldnesses enter, because my Will is Light and contains all possible enjoyments. The human will, on the other hand, is nothing but a portion of darkness and completely full of loathsome things.

Then, if the soul is already in my Volition, before entering and by the mere contact with my Volition, the light has dissipated her portion of darkness in order to change it into my Light. The heat has dissipated her coldness and her aridity; the divine enjoyments have taken away her disgusting things, and my Happiness has freed her from all unhappiness."

April 5, 1908

All that the Queen Mother Contains Has Its Root and Its Beginning in the FIAT.

Continuing in my usual state, I found myself outside myself in a garden in which I could see the Queen Mother seated on a very high throne. I burned with the desire to climb to the top to kiss her hands; and while I was making the effort to climb up, She came toward me and gave me a kiss on my face. Upon seeing Her, I saw in her interior a sort of globe of light; and within this light was the word FIAT; and from this word descended many different and interminable seas of virtue, of grace, of greatness, of glory, of joys, of beauties and all that our Queen

Mother contains. So everything was rooted in that FIAT, and from that FIAT all her benefits had their beginning.

Oh, omnipotent, fruitful, Holy FIAT! Who can comprehend You? I feel mute. It is so great that I do not know how to say anything; therefore, I had better stop. Then I looked at Her in wonder, and She said to me: "My daughter, all my Holiness has come forth from within the word, FIAT. I did not move, nor take a breath, nor take a step, nor do any other action, if I did not take the strength from within the Will of God. It was my food and my all. This produced for Me a Holiness, riches, glories, honors — not human, but Divine. In this way the soul, the more she is united and fused with the Will of God the more she can call herself Holy, the more she is loved by God; and, because of being more loved, so much more is she favored by Him, because the life of that soul is nothing else but the product of the Will of God. And if she is one, single thing with Him, could He help but love her?

Therefore, one should not look at the much or the little that is done, but instead, whether it is willed by God, because God looks more at the little act, if it is according to his Will, than at the great act, without It."

April 8, 1908

For Him Who Lives in the Divine Will, It Is Always Continual Communion.

I was displeased for not being able to receive Communion every day; and my Good Jesus, upon coming, said to me: "My daughter, I do not want you to be displeased over anything. It is true that it is a great thing to receive Communion daily. But

33

how long does this close union of the soul with Me last? At the longest, a quarter of an hour.

The only thing that should matter to you is that you dissolve your Will completely in Mine, because for him who lives in my Will, it is intimate union, not just for a quarter of an hour but always, always. Since my Will is in continuous Communion with the soul, not only once a day, but every hour, every moment, it is always Communion for him who lives in my Will."

May 3, 1908

Effects of the Circulation of the Divine Volition in the Soul

Continuing my usual state, as soon as I felt Our Lord next to me, He said to me: "My daughter, in the soul that does my Will, my Volition circulates in all her being, just as the blood circulates in her; so she is in continual contact with Me, with my Power, with my Wisdom, with my Charity, with my Beauty, and thus takes part in all that is Mine.

No longer living on her own Will, her will lives in Mine. And just as my Will circulates in her will, her will circulates in all my Being. I continually feel its contact, and feeling Myself continually touched by the soul... you cannot comprehend how much love I feel for her, how much I want to favor her and hear her in all she asks of Me. And if she were to be denied anything, I would be denying it to Myself, because, in the final analysis, living in my Volition she does not ask for anything but what I want. This is what she wants and the only thing that makes her happy, as much for herself as for others, because her life is more in Heaven than on earth. This is the fruit that my Will produces: to beatify the soul ahead of time."

January 30, 1909

The Why

Continuing in my usual state, I found myself outside myself; and I seemed to see a soul from Purgatory whom I knew; and I said to her: "Tell me, what is my state before God? I am so afraid, especially for the state in which I find myself." She said to me: "You need to know very little to know if you are in a good or a bad state: if you value suffering, you are in a good state; if you do not value it, you are in a bad state. Because he who values suffering, values God; and valuing Him, he can never make Him unhappy. For the things that are valued are esteemed and guarded with care, more than oneself. And can it be possible that one would wish himself evil? So, then, it is impossible that, valuing God, you could make Him unhappy."

After this, Blessed Jesus came and said to me: "Daughter, in almost all the events that happen, creatures repeat and always say: And why? And why? And Why? Why this sickness? Why this state of soul? Why this punishment? And so many other why's. The explanation of the why is not written on earth but in Heaven, and there all shall read it. Do you know what the why is? It is egoism which gives continual food to self-love. Do you know where the why was created? In Hell. Who was the first to pronounce it? A devil. The effects that the first why produced were the loss of innocence in Eden itself, the war of the implacable passions, the ruin of many souls and all the evils of life. The history of the why is very long. It is sufficient to tell you that there is no evil in the world that does not bear the mark of the why. The why is the destruction of Divine Wisdom in souls. Do you know where the why will be buried? In Hell, to make all the lost souls restless forever, without ever giving them peace. The cunningness of the why is to wage war against souls, without ever giving them rest."

March 23, 1910

To Live in the Divine Will Is More than to Receive Sacramental Communion.

While finding myself in my usual state and lamenting his privations, Jesus came right away and said to me: "My daughter, I recommend that you never go out of my Will, because my Will contains such power that It is a new baptism for the soul. It is, moreover, more than Baptism itself. For in the sacraments my grace is received in a limited way, whereas in my Will, all the fullness of grace is received. In Baptism, Original Sin is taken away, but the passions, the weakness remain. On the other hand, in my Will, by destroying its own will, the soul destroys her passions, her weakness, and all there is that is human, and lives on the Divine virtues, strength, and all the Divine qualities."

I, upon hearing this, said to myself: "Soon He will say that his Will is more than Sacramental Communion Itself." Then He immediately added: "Right! Right! Because Sacramental Communion lasts a few minutes. It is temporary. My Will, on the other hand, is perennial Communion. Even more, it is eternal, and it is eternalized in Heaven. Sacramental Communion is subject to obstacles because of illness or necessities, or on the part of those from whom It should be administered. The Communion of my Will, however, is not subject to any disturbance. If only the soul wants It, it is all done! No one can hinder her from having so great a good — a good that forms the happiness of Heaven and earth — neither the demons, the other creatures, nor my own Omnipotence! The soul is free; no one has the right over her, especially with respect to a soul living in my Will. That is why I want so badly for my creatures to take my Will. This is what matters most to Me, what interests Me most.

And nothing else interests Me so much, not even the most holy things. Only when I obtain that the soul live on my Will do I feel triumphant, because in this is contained the greatest good there can be in Heaven and on earth."

November 1, 1910

The Consummation in the Unity of Wills Forms the Supreme Unity.

Continuing in my usual state, as soon as my Blessed Jesus came, He said to me: "My daughter, the Supreme Unity is when the soul arrives at such an intimate union with my Will as to consume any shadow of her volition, such that it cannot be discerned which is my Volition and which is her own. Then my Volition is the life of this soul, such that whatever I dispose, whether concerning her or concerning others, in all she is content. Everything seems suitable to her: death, life, the cross, poverty, etc. — she sees everything as her own, and as being useful to her to maintain her life. She gets to the point in which even chastisements do not scare her. Rather, in everything she is content with the Divine Volition, so much so that it seems to her that if I want it, she wants it; and if she wants it, the Lord does it; and I do what she wants, and she does what I want.

This is the final phase of the consummation of your will in Mine which I have asked of you so often, but which obedience and charity to your neighbor have not permitted you, so much so that many times I have yielded to you and have not chastised. But you have not yielded to Me. And because of that I have been obliged to hide Myself from you to be free when Justice forces Me and when men finally provoke Me to take the scourge in my hand to chastise the people. If I were to have you with

Me, with my Will, in the act of scourging, I would have diminished the scourge, because there is no power greater, either in Heaven or on earth, than a soul who in everything and for everything is consumed in my Will. This soul is able to debilitate Me, and she disarms Me as she pleases. This is the Supreme Unity. There also exists the poor and lowly union in which the soul is resigned to my Will. Yes, but such a soul does not see my dispositions as her own, as her life. Neither is she happy in my Will; nor does she lose her will in Mine. I see that one, yes; but she does not manage to enamor Me, nor does she cause Me to become enchanted with love for her, as happens with the one who lives in the Supreme Unity."

March 15, 1912

The Divine Will Is the Sanctity of Sanctities.

Continuing in my usual state, I felt a tremendous desire to do the Most Holy Will of Blessed Jesus; and, upon arriving, He said to me: "My daughter, my Will is the Sanctity of Sanctities. Therefore, the soul that does my Will according to the perfection that I teach you, that is, on earth as It is in Heaven, no matter how little, unknown, or ignorant she may be, she will surpass all the other Saints despite their prodigies, striking conversions and miracles. Moreover, the souls who do my Will, as in my Third 'FIAT,' are the queens; and all the others are as if they were at their service. The souls that do my Will in this manner appear as though they do nothing, yet they do everything. Because by remaining in my Will they act divinely, secretly and in a surprising way. Such souls are lights that illuminate, winds that purify, fire that burns, miracles that make miracles occur because it is in these souls that the power to perform them resides. Whereas those doing the miracles are only channels. Thus they are the feet of the missionary, the tongue of the preacher, the strength of the weak, the patience of the infirm, the rule and obedience of subjects, the tolerance of those calumniated, the firmness in dangers, the heroism of heroes, the courage of the martyrs, the sanctity of the saints; and it is like this in everything; because, by remaining in my Will, they participate in all the good that can exist in Heaven as well as on earth.

"Behold, this is why I am able to say that they are my true Hosts, but living Hosts, not dead. For the accidents that form the Host (Eucharist) are neither full of life, nor do they affect my Life; but the soul who remains in my Divine Will is full of life; and in doing my Will she affects and participates in all that I do. This is why these consecrated Hosts of my Will are more dear to Me than my own Sacramental Hosts. And if I have reasons for existing in my Sacramental Hosts, it is to form these Living Hosts of my Will. My daughter, the pleasure that I take in my own Will is so great that only on hearing It mentioned I become elated with joy and call all of Heaven to make merry. Imagine for yourself what it will be like for those souls who do my Will. I find all happiness in them, and I give all happiness to them. Their life is the life of the Blessed. Only two things do they seek, desire, and long for: my Will and Love. They have nothing else to do; and, doing this, they do everything. Even their very virtues remain absorbed in my Will and in my Love. Thus their virtues no longer have anything to do with them, because my Will contains, possesses, and absorbs all, but in a divine way, in an immense and interminable way. This is the life of the Blessed!"

March 20, 1912

All That Matters Is to Give Oneself Entirely to Jesus and to Do His Will in All Things.

Finding myself in my usual state, my always amiable Jesus let Himself be seen all afflicted, and He said to me: "My daughter, they don't want to understand that all that matters is to give oneself entirely to Me and to do my Will in all things. When I have obtained this, I Myself go forth impelling souls, saying to each one: 'My child, take this delight, this comfort, this consolation, this rest... 'But the difference lies in that before giving herself entirely to Me, if the soul took these licit satisfactions, they were human acts; but, afterwards, they become divine actions; and I, seeing that these are now Mine, they no longer cause Me to be jealous. And I say to Myself: 'If she takes this licit pleasure, she takes it because I want it. If she conducts matters or business with others, if she licitly converses... it is because I desire it. And if I did not desire it, she would be disposed and ready to leave everything.' And because of this I put things at her disposal, since all she does is an effect of my Will and no longer her own.

"Tell Me, my daughter, what have you lacked since you have given yourself entirely to Me? I have given you my delights, my pleasures, and all of Myself for your contentment; and this— in the supernatural order. Neither have you lacked anything in the order of faith: Confessors, communions... and everything else. And what is more, you desiring only Me did not want the Confessors so frequently; but I, wanting you to abound in everything, have not always listened to you when you have wanted to deprive yourself for love of Me.

"Daughter, what sorrow my Heart feels in seeing that they do not want to understand this, not even those souls that are said to be very good...!"

April 23, 1912

In the Divine Will the Soul Equals Jesus in His Love.

Finding myself in my usual state, my sweet Jesus came and said: "My daughter, sometimes I permit a fault in a soul who loves Me to bring her closer to Me and to compel her to do greater things for my glory. The more I give her, permitting this same fault so as to have more compassion on her miseries and to love her more and to fill her with my charism, the more I lead her to do great things for Me. These are the excesses of my Love.

"My daughter, my Love for the creature is great. Do you see how the light of the sun invades the earth? If you could divide that light into many particles, you would hear my melodious voice in these particles of light; and they would repeat to you one after the other: 'I love you; I love you; I love you... ,' in such a way that they would not give you time to number them; and you would remain always drowned in that Love. And in reality I love you. I tell you I love you in the light that fills your eyes; I love you in the air you breathe. I love you in the whispering of the wind that touches your ear. I love you in the warmth and cold your body feels. I love you in the blood that flows through your veins. I love you in the beating of your heart. My heartbeat tells you I love you. I repeat my 'I love you' in every thought of your mind; I love you in every movement of your hands; I love you in every step of your feet; I love you in every word, because nothing happens, either inside or outside of you, that is not joined to an act of my Love towards you; so one 'I love you' of Mine does not wait for the other... and of your 'I love you's' — how many are for Me?"

I remained confused. I felt bewildered and deafened on hearing, inside as much as outside of me, the innumerable choruses of all the "I love you's" of my sweet Jesus, before which all my "I love you's" were so small and limited. Accordingly, I said to Him: "Oh my lovable Jesus, who could ever equal You?" But in spite of all I have said it seems I have said nothing of all that Jesus was making me understand. Then Jesus responded to me: "My Divine Will! The true sanctity lies in doing my Will and to reorder all things in Me; and just as I have everything in order for the creature, so the creature should reorder all things for Me and in Me; and my Will brings order to everything."

June 9, 1912

There Are No Deaths in the Divine Will.

I felt somewhat grieved as I was saying to my always amiable Jesus: "When will you take me with you? Oh, hurry, Jesus, make death take me away from this life so it can reunite me with You in Heaven!" Then Jesus said to me: "My daughter, for the soul that does my Will and lives in my Will there is no death. Death is for those who do not do my Will, because they must die to many things: to themselves, to passions, to the world. But whoever does my Will has nothing to die for because she is already accustomed to living the ways of Heaven. For her, death is nothing more than leaving her rags, like one who leaves her poor clothing to be clothed with the vestments of a king to leave the exile and arrive at the fatherland. This is because the soul who does my Will is not subject to death, has no judgment; and her life is eternal. What death should have done, love has done in anticipation; and my Will has reordered her completely in Me, in such a way that I don't have anything for which to judge her. Therefore, stay in my Will; and when you least expect it, you will find yourself in my Will in Heaven."

July 4, 1912

The Divine Will Must Be the Tomb of the Soul.

This morning after Communion I was saying to my always amiable Jesus: "To what state I have been reduced, it seems that everything is fleeing from me: sufferings, virtues, everything...!" Then Jesus said to me: "My daughter, what is wrong? Do you want to waste time? Do you want to leave your nothingness? Take your place — in your nothingness — so that THE ALL can have Its place in you. You must know that everything must die in my Will: sufferings, virtues, everything. My Will must be the tomb of the soul. Just as in the tomb nature is consumed until in reality it disappears; from that same consummation it will arise to a new and more beautiful life. So the soul buried in my Will, like inside a tomb, will die to suffering, to her virtues, to her spiritual goods and will rise in everything to the Divine Life.

"Ah, my daughter, it seems as though you want to imitate the worldly who are absorbed in what is temporal and ending, and do not consider what is eternal! My love, why don't you want to learn to live only in my Will? Why don't you want to live the life of Heaven even while you are on earth? My Will is Love and It is what never dies. Therefore, for you the tomb should be my Will; and the gravestone that should enclose you, without giving you any hope of leaving, is Love. Besides, each thought about one's self, even with respect to the very virtues, is always a gain for oneself and an escape from the Divine Life. To the contrary, if the soul thinks only of Me she takes within herself the Divine Life; and, taking the Divine Life, she leaves her human life and takes all possible goods. Have we understood each other?"

August 14, 1912

With His Hidden Life, Jesus Sanctified and Divinized Every Human Action.

Finding myself in my usual state, my ever loving Jesus said to me: "My daughter, in order for the soul to be able to forget herself, everything she does or has to do must be done as if I wanted to do it in her. If she prays, she should say: 'It is Jesus who wants to pray, and I pray together with Him.' If she works: 'It is Jesus who wants to work; it is Jesus who wants to walk; it is Jesus who wants to eat; who wants to sleep; who wants to get up; who wants to enjoy Himself.' And it should be like that in everything for the rest of her life, excluding errors. Only in this manner is the soul able to forget herself. For not only will she do everything because I want it; but, because I want to do it, she will need Me."

Afterwards I was working and thinking: "How is it possible that while I work it is Jesus who works in me, and it is He who wants to do this work?"

And Jesus: "It is really I; it is my fingers that work in yours. My daughter, when I was on earth didn't I humble Myself working with wood, hammering nails, helping my foster father, Joseph, in his carpentry labors? And while I was doing that, with those same hands and fingers, I was creating souls, while calling others to another life. I was divinizing all human actions; I was sanctifying them, giving divine merit to each. Through the movements of my fingers I was calling all the movements of your fingers as well as all other creatures. And if I saw them laboring for Me, because they wanted Me to perform these acts with them, I would continue my life of Nazareth in them. And due to them I felt, as it were, refreshed in the sacrifices and humiliations of my hidden life, while I offered them the merit of my own Life.

"Daughter, the hidden life which I practiced at Nazareth is neither known nor valued by men. With the exception of my Passion, however, there was no greater good I could have accomplished. By lowering Myself to perform all those little acts that men perform in their daily lives such as eating, sleeping, drinking, working, lighting the fire, sweeping — acts that everyone does — I placed in these souls a divine money of an infinite value. For if it was my Passion that redeemed them; it was my hidden Life that courted their every human action, even the most indifferent, with divine merit and infinite value.

And while you are working — working because I want to work — look how my fingers are in yours. And, at the same moment I work in you, to how many do my hands bring to the light of this world? How many do I call and how many others do I sanctify, correct, chastise, etc.? You, then, are also here with Me to create, to call, to correct, and more. And since you are not working alone, neither am I in all my works. Could I have given you a greater honor?"

But who can express what I have understood, namely, the good that one is able to do for himself and others by doing all things because Jesus wants to perform them in us? My mind is beginning to lose sight, and so I end here.

December 14, 1912

Whoever Is Praying for All in the Divine Will Receives for Herself the Love that God Has for Everyone.

This morning my always amiable Jesus, as He was coming, was tying me with a thread of gold saying: "My daughter, I don't want to tie you with ropes and chains. With those who are rebellious, one uses locks and iron chain. But with the docile, those who don't want any life other than my Will and do not take any nourishment than my Love, hardly one thread is needed to have them united with Me. And many times I don't even use this thread, for they are so inside of Me that they form one thing with Me. And if I use it, it is only to amuse Myself."

And while Jesus would tie me I found myself in the interminable ocean of his Will and, consequently, in all creatures. And I was thinking in the mind of Jesus, in the eyes of Jesus, in his mouth, in his Heart; and, consequently in the mind, in the eyes, and in everything else of the creatures; and I wanted do all that Jesus did. Oh, how with Jesus one embraces everything; no one remains excluded!

Afterwards, Jesus added: "Whoever is in my Will, embracing everything, praying and repairing for everyone, takes in herself the Love that I have for everyone. In this way she encloses within herself all the Love I have for everyone. The more I love her, the more dear she is to Me and the more beautiful; and so she leaves everyone behind her." Then I, having read that whoever is not tempted is not loved by God; and since it seemed to me that it had been a long time since I experienced temptation, I told Jesus, and He said to Me: "My daughter, whoever is totally in my Will is not subject to temptation, because the devil does

46

not have the power to enter in my Will; and not only this but the devil himself does not want to enter because my Will is light, and the soul in the presence of this light would discover his cunningness and would mock him. And he does not tolerate this ridicule, for it is more terrible than Hell itself. So with all his strength he flees. But try to leave from my Will, and you will see how many enemies will fall upon you. Whoever is in my Will always holds high the banner of victory, and none of her enemies dare to face this impregnable banner."

February 5, 1913

Whoever Doesn't Do the Will of God Robs Everything.

This morning my always amiable Jesus came and said to me: "My daughter, whoever doesn't do my Will has no reason to live on earth; his life has no purpose. He is without means and without any end. He is the same as a tree that doesn't know nor can produce any fruit, or worse, produces poisonous fruit that poisons itself more and also whomever might imprudently eat it. This tree does nothing else but rob the hard work of the farmer who with his effort and sweat aerates the soil around it. Thus the soul that doesn't do my Will has the continual attitude of stealing from Me and converting what she takes into poison. So she is always around Me only to steal. She robs the work of Creation, of Redemption and Sanctification. She robs from Me the light of the sun, the nourishment she receives, the air she breathes, the water that quenches her thirst, the fire that warms her, the soil she steps on, because all of this belongs to whoever does my Will. All that is Mine is hers. But whoever doesn't do my Will has no rights, and that is why I feel continually robbed. So whoever doesn't do my Will should be considered as a noxious and fraudulent foreigner, and that is why it is necessary to chain him and throw him into the deepest prisons." Saying this He disappeared.

September 25, 1913

For How Much Union the Soul Has With the Divine Will, So Much More is She Sanctified and the more the Sacraments Produce Their Effects.

Having told the Confessor that Jesus had told me that the Will of God is the center of the soul and that this center is in the depth of the soul and that like the sun, expanding its rays, gives light to the mind, sanctity to the actions, strength to the steps, life to the heart, power to the word and to everything. And not only this, but this center of the Will of God, while it is within us so as always to be at our disposition, is always before and behind us, at our right and left, and everywhere, and will be our center even while in Heaven, never leaving us separated or alone even for a minute. The Confessor, however, said that our center is the Blessed Sacrament.

Then Blessed Jesus came and said to me: "My daughter, I had to accomplish this in a manner that sanctity would be accessible and attainable to everyone, except for whom did not want it, in all conditions, in all circumstances and in all places. It is true that the Blessed Sacrament is the center, but, who instituted it? Who subjugated my Humanity to be enclosed in the brief circle of a Host? Wasn't it my Will? Therefore, my Will always has the supremacy over all. Now then, if the All is in the Eucharist, then the Priests, who call Me from Heaven into their hands and who are more in contact with my Sacramental Body and Blood than anyone, should be the most holy, the most kind. But many times they are the most wicked. Poor Me. How they treat Me in the Most Blessed Sacrament! And so, many souls who receive Me, maybe every day, should be Saints if the Center of the Eucharist would be sufficient. Deplorably, however, they stay always in the same place: vain, quick to anger, obstinate, etc. Poor center of the Blessed Sacrament, how I remain dishonored!

Consider, on the other hand, a mother of a family who does my Will and because of her condition cannot — although she would like to — receive Me every day. She is patient, charitable, and carries within her the perfume of my Eucharistic virtues. Ah, is it perhaps the Sacrament or my Will, to which she has submitted, that has her subjugated and which provides the Blessed Sacrament? Moreover, I tell you that the very Sacraments produce their fruits according to how souls submit to my Will. And they produce their effects depending upon the union these souls have with my Will. And, if there is no union with my Will, they will receive Me; but they will remain fasting. They will go to Confession but will remain always filthy. They will come to my Sacramental Presence; but if our wills are not in accord, I will be for them as if dead, because it is only my Will in the soul who subjects herself to It, that produces all goods and gives life to the very Sacraments. And those who do not understand this are still children in Religion."

October 2, 1913

The 'I Love You' of the Soul in the Divine Will

Continuing my usual state, Blessed Jesus let Himself be seen inside of me, but so fused with me that I would see his eyes in mine, his mouth in mine, and, in the same way all his body. And while I was seeing Him like this, He said to me: "My daughter, see how I fuse Myself and make Myself one sole thing with the soul who does my Will. I make Myself her own life, because my Will is inside and outside of her. You can say that It is like the air she breathes which gives life to everything in her. It is like light that makes everything be seen and understood; It is heat that warms, fecundates, and makes things grow; It is heart that beats, hands that work, feet that walk. And when the human will unites with my Will, my Life is formed in the soul."

Afterwards, having received Communion, I was telling Jesus: "I love You", and He told me: "My daughter, do you really want to love Me? Say: 'Jesus, I love You with your Will.' And since my Will fills Heaven and earth, your love will surround Me everywhere and your 'I love You' will reverberate high in the Heavens, and in the depths of the abysses; and so, if you want to say: 'I adore You, I bless You, I praise You, I thank You...' you will say it united in my Will; and you will fill the Heavens and earth with adorations, blessings, praises, and thanksgiving in my Will. These are simple things, easy and immense.

"My Will is everything, as much as my very own attributes. And what are they? — a simple act of my Will. So then, if Justice, Goodness, Wisdom, Fortitude make their course, my Will precedes them, accompanies them and puts them in position to act. In sum, they do not move one tiny bit from my Will. Because of this, whoever takes my Will takes everything. What is more, she can say that her life is ended, along with her weakness, temptations, passions, and miseries; because for whoever does my Will, all things lose their rights, since my Will has the primacy over everything and rights to everything."

November 18, 1913

As the Soul Has Greater Connection with the Divine Will, So Much More Does the Cross Produce Its Good Effect in the Soul and Sanctify Her.

I was thinking of my poor state and how even the cross is banished from me. And Jesus in my interior said to me: "My daughter, when two wills are opposed to each other, one forms the cross for the other. So it is with Me and creatures: when their will is opposed to Mine, I form their cross and they form Mine.... Thus I am the long shaft that runs vertically along the cross; and they the short shaft, both of which, when crossing each other, form the cross. Now when the soul's will unites itself with Mine, the shafts no longer remain crossed, but united to each other. Hence the cross is no longer a cross. Do you understand? What is more, I sanctified the Cross, the Cross did not sanctify Me. Therefore, it is not the Cross that sanctifies; rather it is the union to my Will that sanctifies the Cross. Accordingly, even the Cross can bring about good only insofar as it keeps itself connected with my Will. And not only this, but the Cross sanctifies, crucifying only a part of the person; whereas nothing escapes my Will. It sanctifies everything, crucifying the thoughts, the desires, the will, the affections, the heart, everything. And my Will, being Light, makes the soul see the necessity of this complete sanctification and crucifixion in such a way that she herself incites Me to want to complete the work of my Will within her. The Cross, therefore, and the other virtues, are content as long as they possess only a part of the creature. And if they succeed to nail the creature with three nails, they make merry and sing their triumph. Instead, my Will, not knowing how to let a work go by until it is completed, is not content with only three nails but wants to use as many nails for the many acts of my Will that I dispose in the creature."

November 27, 1913

The Divine Will Is the Highest Point that Can Exist in Heaven or on Earth.

My ever loving Jesus continued to speak of his Most Holy Will: "My daughter, the creature acquires as many parts of Me within himself for as many complete acts of my Will that he accomplishes. And the more he draws from my Will, the more light he acquires, whereby forming within himself a sun. And since this sun is formed by the light that has been taken from my Will, the rays of this sun are joined to the rays of my Divine Sun. Accordingly, one is reflected in the other; and they dart one another. And while they are doing this, the sun which my Will has formed within the soul grows larger." And I: "Jesus, we are always here in your Will; it seems that You wish to speak about nothing else."

And Jesus: "My Will is the highest point that can exist in Heaven and on earth. And when the soul has arrived at that point, she has arrived at everything and has done everything. Nothing else remains for her except to dwell in these heights, to enjoy them and to comprehend ever more deeply my Will, which is not yet well comprehended either in Heaven or on earth. You have yet time to remain here because you have comprehended little, and there remains a lot for you to understand. My Will is so great that whoever does It can call himself 'god of the earth.' And just as my Will forms the beatitude of Heaven, so these 'gods' who do my Will form the beatitude of the earth and of those who are close to them. And there is no good that exists on the earth that is not attributed to these 'gods' of my Will, either directly or indirectly, and everything must be attributed to them. Just as in Heaven there is no happiness that does not issue from Me, so on earth there is no good that exists that does not come from them."

March 8, 1914

There Is No Good that the Soul United to the Divine Will Does Not Carry with Her at Death.

Continuing in my usual state, my ever loving Jesus did not stop speaking to me about his Most Holy Will. I will say what little that I remember. Now I wasn't feeling very well when Blessed Jesus came and said to me: "My daughter, those who live in my Will can claim all that I do as their very own. And this is because the soul's will, having given itself to Me, remains so identified with Me that she does everything that my Will does. Therefore by living and dying in my Will, there is no good that she does not carry with her because there is no good that my Will does not contain. And my Will is the life of all the goods accomplished by the creatures.

"Whereby, dying to this life, the soul in my Will carries within herself all the celebrated Masses, all the prayers and the good works that are performed, since they are all fruits of my Will. However, they are much less in comparison with the action of my Will Itself, which the soul carries within herself as her own. One instant of this action of my Will is enough to surpass all the actions of all creatures, past, present and future.

"Wherefore the soul that dies in my Will acquires a beauty beyond all beauty. And nothing else can compare with her, neither height, nor riches, nor sanctity, nor wisdom, nor love. Nothing, nothing can compare with her, nothing can equal her. Thus the soul that dies fused in my Will, upon making her entry into her Heavenly Homeland, will find not only the doors of Heaven opening up to her but all of Heaven lowering Itself to allow her to enter her celestial dwelling and to honor the action of my Will in her. What then can I tell you concerning the feast and surprise of all the Blessed upon seeing this soul, entirely sealed with the work of the Divine Will. What can be said of this soul that has done everything in my Will, having done every word, thought, and work in my Will? These will be so many suns that will adorn her, each different from the other in light and beauty. And upon seeing in this soul so many divine rivers, the Blessed will be inundated. Heaven, not being able to contain these divine rivers, they will flow upon the earth for the good of souls.

"Ah, my daughter! My Will is the portent of portents; It is the secret for finding light, holiness, riches. It is the secret of all goods. But, if It is not intimately known, It cannot, consequently, be appreciated nor loved as It merits. Appreciate It, then, and love It, and make It known to whoever you see that is disposed."

Another day, while I was suffering, I felt as if I could not do anything; and I felt oppressed by this. And Jesus, embracing my whole being, said to me: "My daughter, don't be troubled. Seek only to remain abandoned in my Will, and I will do everything for you. For only one instant in my Will is worth more than all the good that you could do in your entire lifetime."

I also remember that on another day He told me: "My daughter, he who truly does my Will can say that everything that takes place within him — be it in his soul or body — whatever he feels, whatever he suffers, takes place in Me. Thus he can say: 'Jesus suffers; Jesus is oppressed.' For everything that creatures do to Me reaches the soul who does my Will, for I dwell in that soul. Therefore, if I suffer from the coldness of creatures, my Will feels it; and because my Will is the Life of that soul, it happens that she also feels it. Therefore, instead of being afflicted over this coldness as if it were her own, she ought to stay by Me to console Me and to make reparation for the coldness that creatures send Me. So if the soul experiences distractions, feels oppressed or whatever else, she ought then to stay by Me in order to relieve Me and make reparation to Me, not however envisioning these crosses as her own, but as Mine. Therefore, the soul that lives in my Will will feel many different pains, according to the offenses that creatures commit against Me. They will be felt suddenly and almost surprisingly. She will also experience joys, indescribable consolations. So, if on the one hand she should occupy herself consoling Me and making reparation, she should also enjoy the contentments and joys. Then my Will finds Its compensation without which It would remain afflicted and unable to carry out Its designs."

On another day He said to me: "My daughter, the soul who does my Will will never enter Purgatory because my Will purges the soul of everything. And having held onto her so jealously in life, guarding her in my Will, how could I possibly permit the fires of Purgatory to touch her? And at the most, should she happen to be lacking in some adornment, then my Will, before revealing the Divinity to her, will go about clothing her with all the garments she needs; and then I will reveal Myself."

March 17, 1914

The Soul in the Divine Will Is Inseparable from God.

Continuing in my usual state, my ever loving Jesus continued to manifest Himself throughout my entire being. I possessed all of his limbs, and He, seemingly so happy He couldn't contain his joy, said to me: "My daughter, the soul who does my Will enters to participate in my actions 'ab intra' (from within) the Divine Persons. This privilege is reserved only for the soul who lives in my Will. Not only will she take part in all of our works 'ad extra' (external), but from these she will pass to works 'ab intra.'

"This is why it is difficult for Me not to please those who live in my Will because, by the soul's remaining in my Will, she remains in the intimacy of our Heart, of our desires, of our affections, of our thoughts. Her heartbeats and her breaths are one with Ours. Therefore how great is the happiness she gives Us, as well as the contentments, the Glory, the Love; and all of these, infinite in nature and manner, are in no way different from our Own, because they are our Own. Just as in our eternal Love, One enraptures the Other, with the One forming the contentment of the Other, so much so that many times being unable to contain this Love, these contentments escape to act 'ad extra.' In this manner We become enraptured and contented by this soul who does our Will. Therefore, how can We displease the soul who has pleased Us so much? How can We not love her — and love her as We love Ourselves, not as We love the other creatures — who loves Us with Our very own Love? With this soul there are no veiled secrets. There is no 'Ours' and 'hers', for all is shared in common. And what We are by nature — impecable, etc. — we make the soul by Grace so that no disparity exists between her and Us. And just as We, not being able to contain our Love produce works 'ad extra,' so also, not being able to contain our Love for the soul who does our Will, We send her out of Ourselves and point her out to the people as our favorite, as our beloved one. And it is for her and other similar souls that We shower down goods upon the earth. It is only for love of them that We conserve the earth. Then, afterwards, We enclose that soul within Us to enjoy her because, just as the Divine Persons are inseparable, so also the soul who does our Will is inseparable from Us."

September 25, 1914

The Universal Effect of Prayers Said with Jesus

I was offering my poor prayers to Blessed Jesus as I pondered whom Jesus would best benefit by applying these prayers. Then, benignly, He said to me: "My daughter, prayers that are said together with Me and with my own Will can be given to all, without excluding anyone; and all will participate in their effects as if they had been offered for one soul alone. But each creature receives their effects according to his own disposition. This is the same as in the case of Communion, or my Passion. I give these to each and every creature, but each creature receives their effects according to his or her own disposition. If ten creatures receive their benefits, the fruits to each are no less than if only five received their benefits. Such is the nature of prayers said together with Me and in my Will."

October 29, 1914

Only in the Divine Will Can a Creature Make Acts of Love, Praise and Thanksgiving that Are Complete and Perfect.

I was lamenting with Jesus over his privations, and my poor, oppressed heart, delirious and full of foolish thoughts, said: "My Love, what is this? Have You forgotten that I cannot be without You? I must be with you either on earth or in Heaven. Must I remind You of this? If You wish to be silent, asleep or angry, then do so, but only as long as You are with me. I feel that You have expelled me from your Heart! Ah! How can You have had the heart to do this?"

As I said these and other foolish things, my sweet Jesus, moving within me, said: "My daughter, be calm, I am here. You insult Me when you say that I have expelled you from my Heart. I have you in the very depths of my Heart, held so close to Me that all my Being flows within you; and your being flows within Me. Therefore, you would do better to be attentive lest any of this, my Being, which flows within you, escape you. See to it, rather, that each one of your acts is united with my Will, because my Will contains acts that are complete. One act of my Will is enough to create a thousand worlds, all perfect and complete. I don't need to perform any subsequent acts. One act is sufficient to accomplish everything. Consequently, when you perform the simplest act, united with my Will, you give Me a complete act of love, of praise, of thanksgiving, of reparation, of everything... in fact everything is enclosed within that act, even to the extent that you enclose Me within that act; and you give Me to Myself. Ah, yes! Only those acts united with my Will can stand before Me.

Only acts that are perfect and complete give honor and satisfaction to a perfect Being, a Being who does not know how to perform incomplete acts; and only in my Will can a creature find such complete and perfect acts. Outside of my Will, no matter how good the creature's acts, they will always be imperfect and incomplete because a creature needs subsequent acts to complete and perfect a work, if in fact the creature ever does perfect it. For this reason I see everything that a creature does outside of my Will as nothing. Therefore my Will must be your life, your norm, your all. Thus, enclosing my Will within you, you shall be in Me and I in you; and you will not be concerned with saying that I have expelled you from my Heart."

December 17, 1914

The Divine Will forms in the Soul the True and Perfect Consecration and Renders It a Living Host.

Continuing in my usual state, I was very distraught from being deprived of Jesus. After much waiting on my part, He finally came and manifested Himself in all of my poor self, to such an extent that it seemed to me I was but his outer garment. Then, breaking his silence He said:

"My daughter, you too can form hosts and consecrate them mystically. Do you see the vestments that cover me in the Sacrament? They have the accidental appearances of bread and wine. But the Life which exists in this Host is my Body, Blood, Soul and Divinity; and that which gives it life is the action of my Supreme Will. And this Will produces the Love, the reparation, the immolation and all the rest that I do in the Sacrament, which cannot deviate even one iota from my Will. Nothing comes forth from Me that is not preceded by my Will. So you, too, may form the host: the material object entirely made by humans. You, too, have a material body and a human will. And if you keep this body and will of yours pure, straight and separated from even the shadow of sin, then you will be providing the accidental clothing I need to enable me to consecrate Myself and live hidden in you. But this is not enough. This alone would be like an unconsecrated host. No, you need my Life; and my Life is composed of Sanctity, Love, Wisdom, Power. And the driving force of all this is my Will. Therefore, after you have prepared the host, you must make your will die in that host. You must, as occurs in the preparation of a host, bake it well, very well, so that it will not come to life again. Then you must enter your entire being into my Will, and my Will which contains all my Life will form the true and perfect consecration.

In this way your human thoughts will no longer have life, and in their place you will have the thoughts of my Will. This will consecrate my Wisdom in your mind. You will no longer have life the way humans have it, with all its weakness and inconsistencies. My Will shall form (in you) the consecration of the Divine Life, of the strength, of the firmness and of everything that I am. Every time that your will, your desires and everything that you are and can do immerse themselves in my Will, I will renew this consecration as in a living Host, not in a dead host such as those that do not contain Me; and I will continue my Life in you. But that is not all. In the sanctuaries housing the Sacramental Hosts, all is dead and mute. There is not even a heartbeat or movement of love in response to so much outpouring of my Love. If it were not that I await human hearts to give Myself to them, I would be disconsolate and defrauded in my Love. There would be no point to my Sacramental Life.

Now, if I tolerate all this in the sanctuaries, I will not suffer it in the living Hosts. Besides, in this Sacrament I wish to be fed and nourished, but by my own nourishment. The soul who makes my Will, my prayers, my reparations and my sacrifices her own, gives them back to Me as if they were her own; and I will nourish Myself from this. The soul will unite herself with Me and will be attuned to what I am doing in order to do it together with Me. As she performs My own acts, the soul will give Me her nourishment; and I will be happy. It is only in these living Hosts that I will find the recompense for my solitude, my fasting and everything I suffer in the sanctuaries.

June 17, 1915

Everything The a Soul Does Should Have Its End in the Divine Will.

Finding myself in my usual state I was complaining to Jesus saying: "Jesus, my Life, all is finished, I have nothing left except your fleeting presences, your shadows." Then, interrupting me, Jesus said: "My daughter, everything must have my Will as its final end. When a soul has reached this stage, it has done everything. If a soul has done much, yet has not acted within my Will, then one could say that she has done nothing. I take account of everything that ends in my Will. Since it is as if my own Life were involved in the acts performed by souls in my Will, it is only to be expected that I be aware of even the smallest things. I am aware of them even when they are so small as to be considered 'nothings' because I feel the smallest act the creature does in my Will, it being done by first taking it from my Will and then acting.

And since my Sanctity, my Power, my Wisdom, my Love and all that I am are included in even the smallest acts, then, when such an act is performed in my Will, I feel in that act done in my Will a repetition of my Life, my works, my words, my thoughts and everything else that is Mine. What more can you desire than to have your acts end in my Will? Everything has its own particular function: the objective of the sun is to spread its light over all the earth. The farmer plants, rakes, and works the land. The farmer feels cold and heat, but that is not his goal. His goal, or function, is to harvest the fruits of his work so that they may nourish him. And so it is with all things. Even though my creations are many, they all revolve around one point, which is the life of man. So also, a soul must make everything end in the singular point of my Will, for this will constitute her life; and from all of this I will take my nourishment."

Later He added: "You and I will experience a very painful period in these sad times. Things will get worse. But you should know that if I remove my wooden cross from you, I will give you the cross of my Will. This cross has neither height nor width, because it is unending. I could not give you a nobler cross. It is not of wood, but of light. And in this light which burns more than any fire, we will suffer together in each creature; and in each creature's tortures we will endeavor to be life for all."

August 24, 1915

Only by Living in the Divine Will Can a Soul Become the Perfect Image and Likeness of God.

I was in my usual state, when my lovable Jesus came; and I gave Him a kiss saying: "My Jesus, if it were but possible, I would give you the kiss that each of your creatures should give You; and so, bringing them all to you, I would bring joy to your Heart."

And Jesus replied: "My daughter, if you wish to give Me a kiss from each of my creatures, kiss Me in my Will because my Will contains the Creative Power; and It can multiply one act into as many acts as desired. Thus you will give Me the pleasure of having been kissed by all. Furthermore, you will receive merit as if you had brought everyone to kiss Me; and all creatures will receive the effects of this kiss according to how well they are disposed. An act done in my Will contains all possible and imaginable goods.

"Let us consider the light of the sun. Its light is one. But this light is multiplied in all the seeing of all creatures, although the light itself is one. It is a single act. Even so, all creatures don't enjoy the light in the same way. Some, whose vision is weak, must partially cover their eyes in order not to be blinded by the light. Others, who are blind, don't benefit from the light at all. This is not the fault of the light, but is rather the fault of the defective vision of creatures.

"Therefore, my daughter, if you wish to love Me on behalf of all, love Me in my Will. Then your love will course through my Will; and, consequently, it will permeate Heaven and earth. I, in turn, will feel Myself repeat your, 'I love you!' all around Me, within Me, and on earth. Everywhere it will be multiplied by as many acts as my Will is capable of performing. Thus you can make Me feel the satisfaction of receiving the love of everyone; though the creature is limited and finite, my Will is immense and infinite.

"How can one explain the words I uttered when I created man: 'Let us make man in our image and likeness'? How can a creature, as inept as he is, be my image and likeness? Only in my Will can he accomplish this. By making my Will his own, a creature can work at the level of the divine; and, by repeatedly performing divine acts, he gradually becomes like Me, eventually even to the point of being transformed into my perfect image.

"This is similar to a child who, by repeating the actions of his teacher, comes to resemble the teacher. The only thing that enables a creature to resemble Me is my Will. It is for this reason that I am now so interested in having creatures make my Will their own, and thereby attain the true goal for which they were created."

November 1, 1915

When a Soul Lives in the Divine Will, It Is Equal To Jesus in Its Capacity to Love.

This morning my sweet Jesus did not make me wait. He came early and, eager and restless, He threw Himself into my arms saying: "My daughter, give Me rest. Help Me find relief for my Love! If my Justice seeks relief, it can exercise itself over all creatures. My Love, on the other hand, finds consolation only in one who loves Me, one who, being wounded by my same Love, deliriously seeks relief in my Love, and constantly asks for more love. Should my Love not find any creature to console Me, my Justice would be mightily ignited and would give its final blow to destroy poor creatures."

And as He spoke, He kissed me over and over again saying: "I love you, but with a Love that is immense. I love you, but with a Love that is incomprehensible. I love you, but with a

Love that is infinite and endless. I love you with a Love that you will never be able to equal." Who can name all the titles that Jesus gave to the Love with which He loves me? To each way He said He loved me, I replied. But not knowing what to say, and not being able to keep up with Him, I said: "Life of mine, You know that I have nothing, that everything I do I take from You, only to return it to You, so that what is mine, being in You, may have continuous activity and life in You, while I remain, as always, nothing. This is why I take your Love and I make it mine, saying: 'I love You with immense and eternal love, with a Love that has no limits or end, and is equal to Yours.' "

I kissed and kissed Him; and, as I repeated my 'I love You,' Jesus would became more quiet and reposed. Later, He returned to let me see his Most Holy Humanity wounded, lacerated, disjointed, and all bloody. I was horrified... and Jesus said: "My daughter, look. I have within Me all the poor, wounded creatures who suffer in war; and I suffer together with them. I want you, too, to partake of these sorrows, for the sake of their salvation." Then Jesus poured Himself into me and made me feel as if I were sometimes agonizing, and then at other times as if I were in mourning. To say it all, He made me feel what He Himself was feeling.

April 1, 1916

Detachment and Fidelity in a Soul Make Her Pulsate As One with Jesus.

This morning my sweet Jesus manifested Himself within my heart, and there our fused hearts beat together. I saw Him, and He said to me: "My daughter, within whoever truly loves Me

65

and in all things does my Will, his heartbeat and Mine become as one to such an extent that I call his heartbeats Mine. Being Mine, I want them all around and even within the beating of my own Heart. They are dedicated to console Me and sweeten Me. All his heartbeats in my own heartbeat will form a sweet harmony that will repeat all my Life and talk to Me of souls, compelling Me to save them.

"But to echo my heartbeat, what a tremendous detachment is needed! One needs to live more a heavenly life than an earthly one, more divine than human. It takes but a shadow, a small thing, to keep a soul from feeling the power, the harmonies and the holiness of my heartbeat, and thus keep it from echoing my own beat in harmony with Me. When that happens I am obligated to be alone with my sorrow or my joy, a sorrow caused by souls who make endless promises to Me, but which, when it comes down to making a decision, defraud Me of these promises."

May 3, 1916

The Soul Who Is in the Divine Will Prays Together with Jesus, Honors the Father and Makes Reparation for Everyone as Jesus.

While I prayed, my lovable Jesus came close. I heard Him praying, and so I listened. Then He said: "My daughter, pray. But pray as I pray. Place yourself entirely within my Will. In my Will you will find God and all creatures; and making all things of the creatures your own, you will give them to God as if given by a single creature because the Divine Will owns them all. You will place at the feet of the Divinity the good acts to

66

bring It honor, and the evil acts to redeem them with the Holiness, Power and Immensity of the Divine Will, from which nothing can escape. That was the Life of my Humanity on earth. No matter how holy my Humanity, I still needed this Divine Will to make complete satisfaction to the Father and redeem the human generations, past, present and future, as well as all their acts, thoughts, words, etc.

"This was done as if in a single act. And in this Holy Will, without anything escaping Me, I took every thought in my mind; and for each one in particular I presented Myself before the Supreme Majesty and gave reparation. In this same Will I descended into the mind of every creature and granted him the good that I had petitioned for his intelligence. In my glances I took the eyes of all creatures. In my voice I included all the creatures' words; in my movements, creatures' movements; in my hands, creatures' works; in my Heart their affections and desires; in my feet their steps; and making all these things Mine in the Divine Will, my Humanity satisfied the Father and rescued poor creatures. The Divine Father was satisfied by all this and could not refuse Me because the Holy Divine Will was also his Will. And could He reject Himself? Certainly not! What is more, in these acts He found perfect Holiness, inaccessible and enrapturing Beauty, supreme Love, immense and eternal acts, and invincible Power. This was the entire life of my Humanity on earth from the first instant of Conception to the exhaling of my last breath, and, afterwards, in Heaven and in the Blessed Sacrament.

"Now, why can't you do this also? Everything is possible in unison with Me for those who love Me. Pray in the Divine Will before the Divine Majesty, and take the thoughts of all creatures enclosed in your thoughts, in your eyes the glances of everyone, in your words, in your movements, in your affections, in your desires, all those of your brothers and sisters. Thus you will repair these acts, and gain for creatures Light, Grace and Love. In my Will you will find yourself enclosed within Me and within all creatures. You will live my Life, pray as I prayed; and the Divine Father will be pleased. All Heaven will say: 'Who is this calling from earth? Who wants to enclose this Holy Will, encompassing all of us within himself?' How much good the earth can obtain when it makes Heaven descend upon it!"

May 25, 1916

Jesus' Working in a Soul Requires the Soul's Response If It Is To Produce Fruits Pleasing to Him.

As I continued in my usual state, I was grieved, especially because Blessed Jesus made me realize that foreign soldiers were invading Italy and such a great butchery was taking place amongst our soldiers that Jesus Himself was horrified to watch. I felt my heart torn asunder by this sorrow and said to Jesus: "Save my brothers, your images, from this lake of blood, and don't allow any soul to fall into Hell..." Realizing that Divine Justice was about to increase its furor against poor creatures, I felt I would die. Then Jesus, as if to distract me from such heartrending scenes, said:

"My daughter, my Love for souls is so great that when a soul decides to give herself to Me, I surround her with abundant grace; I caress her; I prompt her; I make her withdraw within herself; I endow her with perceptible graces, with favors, with inspirations, with heartfelt needs. A soul that finds herself so endowed begins to love Me. She creates a storehouse of prayers and of pious practices in her heart, and decides to grow in virtue. All this creates, as it were, a flowery orchard in the soul. But my Love is not satisfied with just flowers. It also wants fruits. Therefore, it makes the flowers fall; that is, it deprives the soul of any perceptible love, of zeal for anything else, in order to make her fruitful. If the soul is faithful and continues her pious practices and continues growing in virtue, if she disdains all human things, if she does not think of herself but rather of Me, if she puts her trust in Me, then in this way the orchard of the soul gives flavor to her fruits. With the soul's faithfulness she will make her fruits mature, with her courage, tolerance and peacefulness she will make her fruits grow; and they will be plentiful and splendid.

"And I, as a Heavenly Farmer, will harvest these fruits and will nourish Myself with them. Then I will plant another orchard, even more beautiful and florid, in which fruits of heroic proportions will grow. These new fruits will wrest from Me unspeakable graces. But if, on the other hand, the soul is unfaithful and does not put her trust in Me; if she frets and continues to delight in human things, etc., the fruits will be tart, insipid, bitter and infected... and this will only make Me withdraw from the soul in bitterness."

August 6, 1916

Jesus Needs More Souls Who Live in His Will.

As I continued in my usual state, my sweet Jesus came for an instant and said: "My daughter, my Heart feels an irresistible need that more souls live in my Will because these souls are festive places for Me. My Love wants to do good to all souls, but their guilt prevents Me from showering my benefits on them. So I go in search of those souls who live in my Will. Since nothing hinders Me from showering my blessings on them, I do so; and through these souls the individuals and populations which surround them also benefit. Therefore, the greater the number of such souls that exist on earth, the more my Love will be consoled and the more it will pour itself forth to benefit humanity."

August 12, 1916

The Glory of Souls Who Live in the Divine Will on Earth.

As I immersed myself in the Most Holy Divine Will my sweet Jesus said: "My daughter, I only feel compensated for the Creation, the Redemption and the Sanctification of creatures by the souls who live in my Will; and they glorify Me in the manner which creatures should glorify Me. For this reason these souls shall be the jewels of my throne. They shall take for themselves all the satisfactions and the glory which each one of the Blessed will only enjoy individually. These souls will be like queens around my Throne, and all of the Blessed will surround them. And because the Blessed will be like many suns which shine in the Heavenly Jerusalem, those souls who have lived in my Will shall shine in my Sun, shall be fused with my Sun to such an extent that the Blessed will see these souls as if they were in my very Self. For it is only just that, having lived united with Me — with my Will — on earth without having a life of their own, they should have in Heaven a position different from all the rest, and that they should continue living in Heaven the life that they lived on earth, totally transformed in Me and plunged into the ocean of my pleasures."

September 8, 1916

The Soul in the Divine Will Must Repeat What Jesus Did in It.

This morning when I received Communion I felt that my lovable Jesus absorbed me in a special way into his Will, as if I were swimming in Him. But who can say what I felt? I don't have words to express myself... and then Jesus said to me: "My daughter, to the extent that a soul is in my Will, to that extent can she say that she lives my Divine Life on earth. Oh! how it pleases Me when I see a soul enter into my Will to live the Divine Life! It pleases me very much to see souls repeating in my Will those things that my Humanity did in my Will.

"When I instituted the Eucharistic Sacrament and gave Myself in Communion to the Apostles, I gave Communion to Myself in the Will of the Father. In this way I not only repaired everything, but finding in the Divine Will the Immensity, the Omnipresence in everything and in everyone, I embraced all and gave Myself in Communion to all. Then, seeing that many had not taken part in this Sacrament, and seeing the Father offended because they did not want to partake of Life, I gave glory as if all had received Holy Communion. I gave to the Father on behalf of each one of these souls the satisfaction and the glory of a Divine Life. Now you, too, as you receive Communion in my Will, repeat everything, giving Me to all as I wanted to give Myself to all; and you will give Me glory as if all had received Communion. My Heart is softened when it sees that a creature, unable to give Me anything of his own that is worthy of Me, takes my actions as his own, imitates the way I did them; and, to please Me, gives them to Me. I, in turn, feeling gratified, respond to the soul with: 'Bravo, my child! You have done exactly what I did.'

"Then I add: 'Acts done in my Will are the simplest of acts, and because they are simple they can be communicated to all creatures. The sun's light, because of its simplicity, illuminates every eye, but the sun is one. One single act in my Will, just as the most simple light, is diffused in every heart, in all works, in all creatures. But the act is one. My Being, because It is extremely simple is a single act, but an act which contains everything. It has no feet, but It constitutes the step of everyone. It has no eyes, but It is the eye and the light of all. I give life to all, but without any effort, without ever tiring; and I give all creatures the act of being able to work.'

"In like manner, the soul in my Will simplifies herself; and, together with Me, multiplies herself in all and brings good to all. Oh, if only everyone would understand the immense value of acts, even minimal, insignificant acts, done in my Will! They would not let even one single act escape them."

October 2, 1916

Effects of Communion Received by the Soul in the Divine Will.

This morning I received Communion as Jesus had taught me, that is, united in his Humanity and his Most Holy Will. Then Jesus let Himself be seen, and I kissed Him and pressed Him to my heart; and He, returning me the kiss and the embrace, said to me: "My daughter, how happy I am that you have come to receive Me united with my Humanity, to my Divinity and in my Will. You have renewed all that I felt was contained in Me as I received Myself in Communion; and while you would kiss Me and embrace Me, all of Me being in you, you contained all creatures; and I felt the kiss of everyone. Because this was your will, just as it was Mine as I received Myself in Communion to redo and present to the Father all the love of creatures; and in spite of the fact that many would not love Him, the Father recovered in Me the love of all creatures. And having found one in my Will who loves Me, repairs Me, etc., in the name of everyone, because in my Will there is nothing that the soul cannot give Me, I feel Myself being loved by creatures in spite of their offenses; and, because of this, I go inventing stratagems of love around the most hardened hearts to convert them. Only for love of these souls that do everything in my Will do I feel as though enchained and enraptured, and I grant them the prodigies of the greatest conversions."

December 22, 1916

As the Soul Receives Communion and Acts in the Divine Will, She Renews the Fire of Communion and the Acts of Jesus.

Having received Holy Communion I was uniting myself all in Jesus and fusing myself all in his Will. I would say: "I don't know how to do anything nor say anything. That is why I feel the great necessity to do what You do and repeat your same words. In your Will I find present, as in act, the acts that You did when You received Yourself Sacramentally. And I make them mine and repeat them to You..." And in that way I was trying to interweave myself in all that Jesus did as He received Himself Sacramentally. And while I was doing this He said: "My child, whoever does my Will and all that he does he does it in my Will, obliges Me to do with him what he does. Therefore, if he receives Communion in my Will, I repeat the acts that I did when I received Myself in Communion; and I renew the complete fruit of my Sacramental Life. If he prays in my Will, I pray with him and renew the fruit of my prayers. If he suffers, if he works, if he speaks in my Will, I suffer with him and renew the fire of my sorrows. I work and speak with him and renew the fruit of my works and words, and so with all the rest..."

February 24, 1917

On Receiving Communion the Soul Must Be Consumed in Jesus and Give the Complete Glory of the Sacramental Life of Jesus in the Name of Everyone.

Having received Communion, I held my sweet Jesus closely to my heart; and I said to Him: "My Life, how I would like to do what You Yourself did when You received Yourself Sacramentally, so that You can find in me your contentments, your same reparations." Then my always amiable Jesus said to me: "My daughter, in this brief circle of the Host I enclosed everything. And because of this I wanted to receive Myself: to make acts that would glorify the Father worthily for the creatures who would be receiving a God, and I gave creatures the complete fire of my Sacramental Life. In any other manner it would have been incomplete, as much as for the glory of the Father as for the good of the creatures. And because of this my prayers are in every Host, my gratitude and all the rest that is needed to glorify the Father and that creatures owed Me. And if the creature fails, I continue my work, receiving Myself in each soul. Besides, the soul ought to transform herself in Me and be made one with Me. She should make my Life her own, my groanings of Love, my sorrows, my heartbeats of fire, with which I would desire to make her burn. But I do not find anyone who will endure the cost of my flames, and I am reborn in the Host and live, die and am consumed; but I cannot find who would consume herself for Me. And if the soul repeats what I do, then I feel as though she has received Me again; and I find complete glory, divine joys, outpourings of love equal to my own; and I give the grace to the soul to be consummated in my same consummation."

July 4, 1917

Whoever Lives in the Divine Will, Palpitates in the Sacramental Heart of Jesus.

Continuing in my habitual state, I was suffering; and my adorable Jesus came, placing Himself in front of me. It seemed to me that between us there were electrical wires of communication; and He said to me: "My daughter, each pain suffered by the soul is an additional means of communication that the soul acquires, because all the pains that creatures can suffer were first suffered in my Humanity; and they took their place in the divine order. Since the creature is unable to suffer them all, my Kindness communicates them little by little; and as they are communicated, the bond of union with Me grows. And not only do these sufferings produce this effect, but also every good act that the creature can accomplish. That is how the bonds between the creature and me develop."

On another day I was thinking how good it is for others to be in front of the Blessed Sacrament, while I, poor me, am deprived of this blessing. And Blessed Jesus said to me: "My daughter, whoever lives in my Will remains with Me in the Tabernacle and participates in the sufferings, indifferences, and irreverences I suffer from these same souls in my Sacramental Presence. Whoever lives in my Presence has supremacy over all and always has a reserved place of honor. Who, then, receives more, he who is in front of Me or he who is in Me? For he who lives in my Will I do not tolerate even the distance of a small step between him and Me, nor divisions of sufferings or joys. Perhaps I place him on the Cross, but always with Me.

"This is why I always want you in my Love — to give you first place in my Sacramental Heart. I want to feel your heartbeat in Mine... with my same Love and pain. I want to feel your will in Mine which, when multiplied in everyone, may give Me one single act of reparation for all as well as everyone's love. And uniting your will to Mine and making your poor humanity Mine, I can lift it up before the Majesty of the Father as my continuous victim."

July 7, 1917

Everything that a Soul Does in the Divine Will Is As One Ongoing Ever-Present Act.

Being fused into my sweet Jesus, and miserable and lowly as I am, I did not know what to give Him, when my always sweet Jesus consoled me: "My daughter, there is no past or future for those who live in my Divine Will, but rather everything is, as it were, an ongoing act. So, also, everything that I did and suffered is ever-present as an ongoing act; and if I want to give satisfaction to the Father, or benefit creatures, I can do it as if I were offering a current suffering or action. Everything a creature suffers or does in my Will is fused with my sufferings and my acts and becomes as one with them. When a soul wants to give evidence of her love for Me she can take her previous sufferings, which are an ongoing act, and give them to Me to duplicate her love and her reparations towards Me. When I see the ingenuity of a creature who invests his acts, as if in a bank, to multiply them and earn interest on them in order to give Me love and make reparation, then I, not willing to be outdone by his love, and to enrich the creature more abundantly, will give him my sorrows, my manifold acts, as gifts of my Love to make the creature love Me in return."

July 18, 1917

The Soul Who Lives in the Divine Will Lives in Jesus and at His Expense.

Continuing in my usual state, I tried to pour myself entirely into the Holy Will of Jesus and asked Him to pour Himself entirely into me, so that I would no longer be aware of myself, but only Jesus. Then Blessed Jesus came and said: "My daughter, when a soul lives by my Will and does everything in my Will, I feel the soul everywhere: I feel her in my Mind, and her thoughts flow through Mine. And since the life of the intelligence of creatures comes from Me, this life and I diffuse together in their minds. When this soul sees events that offend Me, she feels my pain. I feel the soul in my heartbeat; but more than that, I feel as if there were two heartbeats in one as the soul, empowered by my Love, flows together with Me and loves together with Me. And when I am not loved, this soul loves Me for everyone. She reciprocates my Love and consoles Me. In my desires I feel the desires of the soul who lives in my Will. In my acts, I feel the soul's acts; and so it is with everything. So I can truly say that the soul lives by Me and at my expense."

I replied: "My Love, You do everything in and of Yourself. You don't need creatures. Why, then, do you love so much for creatures to live in and by your Will?" And Jesus said: "It is true that I have need of nothing and that I do everything on my own. But in order to have life, love needs to express itself. A sun doesn't need any light. It has enough light for itself and for others. But if there are other lights, even of the smallest magnitude, let us suppose that the sun would want them as companions to enhance and embellish them. What would you say, then, if those lights, ever so tiny, rejected the sun? Ah! my daughter, when the will is alone it is always sterile. Love that is not expressed languishes and is eventually extinguished. I love creatures so much that I want them united with my Will to make them fertile, to give them a life of love. In this encounter I find release for my Love. I have created creatures to pour out my Love — for this reason alone and for no other. That is my sole desire."

July 25, 1917

Jesus Purifies a Soul on Admitting Her to Live in His Will.

As I continued in my usual state I lamented to Jesus, and asked Him to put an end to so many chastisements. Then Jesus said to me: "My daughter, you lament? Yet these are nothing. The great chastisements are still to come. Creatures have become unbearable. When they are chastised, they rebel even more. They don't even wish to recognize that it is my hand that chastises them. I have almost no other means at my disposal but to exterminate creatures. That will be the only way I will be able to remove from earth so many lives that fill it with stench and kill my growing future generations. Therefore, don't expect an end to chastisements yet, but rather await those that are even worse. Creatures will be inundated with blood."

As I heard this, my heart was torn asunder. Then, desiring to console me, Jesus said: "My daughter, come into my Will to do what I do. Within my Will your acts will be able to flow for the good of all creatures; and you will be able to save them with the Power of my Will, even as they swim in their own blood. Thus you will present them to Me washed by their own blood with the seal of my Will."

I replied: "My Life, I am so bad myself.... How can I do this?" Jesus said: "My daughter, know that the most noble, sublime, and heroic act is to do my Will and to act within my Will. That is why with great fanfare and in great abundance I bestow upon such acts, which have no equal, all my Love and generosity. In order to be able to give a soul who decides to act in my Will this honor, in the process of our two wills encountering each other and fusing themselves into one, I purify her if she is stained. I destroy the thorns of human nature if she is covered by them; and I pulverize any nails — sins—that pierce it. Nothing evil may enter into my Will. What's more, such a soul is invested with all my attributes. They transform her weakness into strength, ignorance into wisdom, misery into riches, and it is like this with all the other attributes. There always remains something of the soul in those acts not done in my Will. But in those done in my Will the soul is stripped of herself, and I completely fill her with Myself."

October 20, 1917

How a Soul Can Form a Host for Jesus

Having received my Jesus in Holy Communion, I reflected on how I might give love for Love. But it was impossible for me to reduce myself, to make myself small, as Jesus does in the Host for love of me. While it is within Jesus' power to do this, it is entirely beyond my capabilities, so my beloved Jesus said to me:

"My daughter, if you are not able to squeeze all of yourself within the brief circle of a Host for my Love, you can do so very easily in my Will in order to form a Host of yourself in my Will. Each act that you do in my Will shall make a Host for Me, and I will feed upon you as you feed upon Me. What is it that forms the Host? My Life in It. What is my Will if not the fullness of my Life? So, you also can make yourself a Host for love of Me. As many acts that you do in my Will so many more Hosts do you make in order to give Me love for Love.

November 20, 1917

The Reason for the Chastisements: Jesus Wants to Make Reappear the Holiness of Living in the Divine Will.

I found myself in a state more painful than usual, yet my ever amiable Jesus came and left like a flash of lightning. He did not even give me time to intercede with Him for the many misfortunes which humanity is experiencing, in particular my beloved country. What a blow to my heart it was for the enemy to invade it. I thought Jesus had told me this beforehand only to make me pray.

But now as I intercede with Him when He appears, He says, "I will be inexorable." I have even insisted, saying to Him: "Don't You want to have some compassion? Don't You see how cities are destroyed and people are naked and hungry? Oh, Jesus, how hard you have become!" And then He said to me: "My daughter, I have no concern for cities, for the grandeur of the earth. My concern is for souls. Cities, churches and all the rest can be rebuilt after they are destroyed. Wasn't everything destroyed in the Flood, and wasn't everything reconstructed? But if souls are lost, it is forever. No one can give them to Me anew. Ah, I cry for souls! For the earth they have forgotten Heaven. I will destroy the earth and make the most beautiful things disappear, which, as traps, hold men bound."

And I replied: "Jesus, what are You saying?" He said: "Courage, don't be anxious, I will proceed. But you come into my Will so that the earth will no longer be your dwelling place. I will be your dwelling. That way you will be protected from everything. My Will can make a soul transparent, so that everything I do will be reflected in her. When I think, my thought is reflected in her mind and becomes light; and her thought, as if it were light, is reflected in Mine. My glances, my words, my acts of Love... as so many lights are reflected in the soul and the soul is reflected in Me so that we are continually reflecting upon one another in constant communication, in reciprocal love. And since I am everywhere the reflections from this soul reach Me in Heaven, on earth, in the Sacramental Hosts, in the hearts of all creatures...."

Always I give light, and these souls give light in return. I give Love, and love is given in return. These souls are my ter-restrial dwelling where I find refuge from the nausea that other creatures produce in Me. Oh, living in my Will...! It pleases Me so much that in future generations I will make all other forms of sanctity disappear, no matter what virtue they are based upon. In their place I will make reappear the sanctity of living in my Will, which is not a human form of sanctity but rather a Divine Sanctity. It will be such a high order of sanctity that, like a sun, it will eclipse the most beautiful stars of the Saints of previous generations. That is why I want to purify the earth because as it is now, the earth is unworthy of such a wonder of Sanctity."

November 27, 1917

In the Sanctity of Living in the Divine Will There Is No Lost Time nor Any Self Interest.

I continue only out of obedience. My ever amiable Jesus wants to continue talking about life in his Most Holy Will. While He speaks of his Most Holy Will, He forgets everything else and He makes me forget myself. Then the soul only feels the need and the goodness of living in his Will. Then, having completed the previous writing (twentieth day of the month) concerning his Will, my sweet Jesus became displeased with me and said: "My daughter, you have not said everything. I want you to leave out nothing I tell you about my Will. Even the smallest details will benefit those who will come later. There have always been different types of sanctities and all kinds of Saints to initiate them. Thus there was a Saint who initiated the sanctity of penitents, another who initiated the sanctity of obedience, another that of humility, and likewise for all the others. I want you now to initiate the sanctity of living in my Will.

My daughter, all the other types of sanctity involve the loss of much time and allow for much personal self-interest. For example, a soul that lives under obedience is subject to the loss of much time. It can talk and talk, and that talking distracts the soul and places the virtue where only I should be. If such a soul is not subject to ever new orders of obedience she loses her tranquility, suffers temptations, etc. Oh, what a loss of time! She never tires of talking about the obstacles in her way and puts her virtue where I belong. Many times such sanctities fade away.

The sanctity of living in my Will, on the other hand, is totally selfless, involves no loss of time; and there is no likelihood that I will be replaced by any virtue, because to live in my Will is to live in Me. This was the sanctity of my Humanity on earth, and that is why I did everything for everyone without the slightest hint of self-interest. Self-interest removes the seal of Divine Sanctity; and it makes it impossible for the soul to be a sun, limiting it to be, at best, only a star, however beautiful it may be.

This is why I want the sanctity of living in my Will. In these sad times this generation needs these suns to warm it, to enlighten it, to nourish it. The lack of self-interest of these terrestrial angels, working only for the good of others, without the slightest self-interest, will open the way in everyone's heart to receive my grace.

Besides, there are few churches and many of them will be destroyed. Often there are no Priests to consecrate Me. Many other times Priests allow unworthy souls to receive Me, or don't make it possible for souls that are worthy to receive Me. Thus my Love meets with obstacles. That is why I want to establish the sanctity of living in my Will. When souls live in this sanctity I will not need Priests to consecrate Me, nor churches, nor tabernacles, nor Hosts, because these souls will be everything: Priests, tabernacles and Hosts; and my Love will be liberated. Every time a soul wishes to consecrate Me she will be able to do so, at any moment of the day or night, wherever the soul may be. Oh, how that primordial Love will find complete expression and satisfaction.

Ah, my daughter, the present generation deserves to be totally destroyed; and if I allow a small remnant to survive, it is only to form these suns, sanctified by living in my Will. These suns, following my example, will restore to Me everything that all creatures — past, present and future — owe Me. Then the earth will give Me true glory, and my 'Thy Will be done on earth as It is in heaven' will be heard and will find fulfillment."

Why Human Acts Performed Outside of the Divine Will Don't Please Jesus

After I received Jesus in the Sacrament I was saying to Him: "I kiss You with the kiss of your Will. You are not satisfied if I give you only my kiss, because you want to receive kisses from all creatures. That is why I give you my kiss in your Will. I find all creatures in your Will; and, being in your Will, I take all their mouths and I kiss You with your Love. Not with my love, but with your own Love do I kiss You, so that You will feel the joy, the sweetness and the tenderness of your own Love on the lips of all creatures; and then, You being attracted by your own Love, I can compel You to give your kiss to all creatures." Who knows how much nonsense I spoke to my lovable Jesus!

Then my sweet Jesus said to me: "My daughter, how sweet it is to see and hear a soul in my Will! Without her knowing it, the soul finds herself at the height of my acts and of my prayers; and, by doing as I did when I was on earth, she places herself at my level. Even in my smallest acts I encompassed all creatures, past, present and future so that I offered to the celestial Father completed, perfect acts on behalf of all creatures. Not even a single breath of a single creature was left outside of my Being. Had it been otherwise, the Father would have been able to take exception as He gazed upon all creatures and all their acts. Had these acts not all been done by Me, nor have come from Me, He could have said: 'You have not done everything for everyone; your work is not complete. I cannot give recognition to all creatures because You have not incorporated them into Yourself. I want to recognize only what You have done.'

"For this reason, in the immensity of my Will, of my Love, and of my Power I did everything for everyone. How can acts not done in my Will please Me, beautiful though they may be? They are always low, human acts, limited acts. Acts done in my Will, on the other hand, are as noble, divine, unlimited, and infinite as my Will. They are similar to my acts; and I ascribe to them the same value, the same love and the same power as my acts. I multiply them in all creatures, and I extend them to all generations throughout time. It doesn't matter that they be small acts; they are still repetitions of my acts, and that is all that is important.

"Furthermore, the soul finds herself not just in a state of humility, in which she still feels something of herself, but rather discovers her true nothingness. Realizing she is nothing, she enters into the All and acts with Me, in Me and like Me, totally stripped of herself. She takes no notice of her own merits, nor of her own interests, but rather is entirely devoted to pleasing Me, giving Me absolute dominion over all her acts, without desiring to know what I do with them. While requesting that I give her this great honor, such a soul has but one concern: to live in my Will. This is why I love her so, why I lavish all my predilection, all my Love, on a soul who lives in my Will. If I love other souls it is in virtue of the Love with which I love these souls, just as the Father loves creatures by virtue of the Love He has for Me."

I said: "Ah, Jesus, how true what you say. When one lives in your Will, one desires to have nothing else, nor to know anything else; and if one wishes to do something it is only because You have done it. One feels the burning desire to repeat your acts. Everything else disappears, and one wishes to do nothing other than this." And Jesus said: "...and I make the soul do everything, and I give her everything."

March 26, 1918

A Soul Is Enriched in as Much as She Enters into the Divine Will

Continuing in my usual state, I was trying to fuse myself in the Divine Will; and my sweet Jesus said to me: "My daughter, every time a soul enters into my Will and prays, acts or suffers, she acquires as many divine embellishments. Therefore, an act done in my Will, or left out of my Will, represents an additional embellishment either acquired or forfeited by the soul. Furthermore, with every new act done in my Will the soul acquires new power, wisdom, love and Divine Sanctity, and as she acquires these characteristics of the divine, she surrenders her human characteristics. When a soul acts in my Will her humanity is, as it were, suspended. Then the Divine Life of my Love takes Its place and acts; and, as It acts in a creature, my Love finds itself unburdened of its desire for expression."

March 27, 1918

When She Lives in the Divine Will a Soul Enjoys All Things in a Divine and Infinite Manner.

I complained to Jesus that I couldn't even hear Holy Mass, and Jesus said: "My daughter, aren't I the sacrifice? When I am sacrificed, the soul that lives with Me in my Will is sacrificed together with Me, not only in one Mass, but in all Masses, from the first to the last. Since she lives in my Will the soul is consecrated in all the Hosts. Never leave my Will and I will take you wherever you want. Furthermore, such an electric current of communication will pass between us that you will not do one act without Me, nor will I do any act without you. Therefore, when you have need of something, such as to hear Mass, enter into my Will and you will immediately find what you seek: as many Masses as you wish, as many Communions as you wish, as much love as you wish. Nothing is lacking in my Will. Not only will you find all things, but you will find them in a divine and infinite manner.

December 27, 1918

These Writings Are Like a Sun that Illuminates Everyone and Will Be the Loss of Those Who Don't Avail Themselves of Them.

These days I have not written anything that Jesus spoke to me because I didn't feel like doing it; so when Jesus came He said: "My daughter, why don't you write? My word is Light. Like a sun it radiates in every eye so that all will have sufficient light to satisfy all their needs. Being even more powerful than a sun, every one of my words can enlighten any mind and inflame any heart. Every one of my words is a sun that emanates from Me. Although now they are useful to you alone, by writing them down you will render them useful to others. When you don't write down my words, you extinguish these suns, you hinder the expression of my Love; and you impede all the good that these suns might do."

I replied: "Ah, my Jesus! Who will ever read, word for word, everything that You are dictating to me?" He replied: "For now this is not your concern. It is my concern. Even if no one were to read these writings word for word, which will not be the case, the many suns of my words will rise majestically taking their place for the good of all. Whereas if you don't write them you keep these suns from rising and thus will do great harm, as much harm as one would do who kept the earth's sun from rising over the horizon. How much harm would this wreak upon the earth? But even this would only harm the earth. On the other hand your failure to write would harm — souls! It is the glory of the sun to glow majestically and gather in the grasp of its light everything and everyone on earth. Only those who fail to avail themselves of this light do not receive its benefits. So also will it be with regard to the suns of my words. It will be my glory to make many different suns arise. It is their loss if any do not avail themselves of the light of these suns."

January 8, 1919

Wars And Persecutions. The Divine Will Transforms the Acts of the Creature into Infinite and Eternal Acts.

Continuing in my habitual state, I was very discouraged by the absence of my Jesus when suddenly He appeared. But He looked sad and tired, searching for comfort in my heart to cover Himself from the grave offenses being committed against Him; and with a sigh He said to me: "My daughter, hide Me! Can't you see how they persecute Me? Have pity on Me! They want to eradicate Me, or at best, give Me the last priority in their lives. Let Me vent my sorrow, for it's been many days since I've talked to you about the destiny of the world, the punishments which in their evil they'll tear out of Me. The pain is concentrated in my Heart, so I want to talk to you about all this, to make you participate and share with Me in the destiny of creatures, to be able to pray, suffer and cry together on their behalf.

"Oh, my daughter, there will be wars among the peoples and death will take many lives, even among Priests! Oh, how many Priests are only masked! I wish to unmask them before the rise of persecution against my Church and the revolution to come; perhaps they will convert at the moment of death; otherwise, if I leave them, under persecution they will remove their masks to become apostates (sectarians) and will become the fiercest enemies of the Church, making their salvation even more difficult."

And so I, very afflicted told Him: "Oh my Jesus, it's painful to hear You talk about these blessed punishments! But the peoples — what will they do without Priests? They are already scarce, and You still want to remove many? Who will administer the Sacraments? Who will teach your Laws."

Jesus added: "My child, don't be so afflicted, the scarcity of numbers is nothing. I will give to just one the grace and strength I give to ten, twenty..., I can supply everything. Many bad Priests are the poison of the people. Rather than do good, they do evil; and what I will do is remove the primary elements that poison the people."

Jesus disappeared; and I remained with a nail in my heart from what He told me, very upset from thinking about the sorrow of my sweet Jesus, the destiny that awaits the poor creatures. Jesus then came back and taking me in his arm told me: "My loved one, take courage, come within Me, come dive into the immense ocean of my Will, of my Love; hide in the uncreated Will and Love of your Creator. My Will has the power to make infinite everything that enters It and to elevate and transform the acts of the creature into eternal acts. What enters my Will acquires the eternal, the infinite, the immense, losing the beginning, the limited, the small. So say loudly in my Will: 'I love You,' and I will hear the melody of my Eternal Love; I will feel the created love hidden in the Uncreated Love; and I will feel loved by the creature with an Eternal, Infinite, Immense Love, a love worthy of Me, which satisfies Me and compensates for all."

Amazed and marveled, I said to Jesus: "Jesus, what are you saying?" And He replied: "My child, don't be surprised; everything is eternal in Me. Nothing has beginning or end. You yourself and the creatures were eternal in my Mind; the Love with which I fashioned all creation, the Love that came forth from Me to endow each and every heart is eternal. How marvelous, then, that the creature, leaving its own will, enters Mine. And the creature, uniting himself to the Love that embraced and loved him from Eternity and uniting with the Eternal Love from which he came, loving Me in his activity, acquires a value and power which are infinite and immense. Oh, how little is known about my Will! That's why It isn't loved or appreciated, and so the creature stays complacent and acts as if his origin were not eternal but temporary!"

Afterwards, I was thinking that I don't even realize when I say ridiculous things. But my gentle Jesus places such light in my mind concerning his Divine Will that I am unable to contain it. Yet, I find no words to express myself. As my mind was getting lost in the light, my Blessed Jesus appeared saying: "To make you understand better what I've told you, just imagine a sun. And this sun releases many little lights, sending them across space, allowing them the freedom to live diffused in creation or to remain in the very sun from which they came... Is it not fair for the little lights that live in the sun, in their actions, in their love, to acquire the heat, the ardor, the power and the immensity of the sun itself? Moreover, they have remained in the sun; they are part of the sun; the sun is their sustenance, and they share the same life of the sun. They neither augment or diminish the sun, because what is immense is not subject to increase or decrease; but it does receive the glory and honor of those lights that return to it, living in it. And all this is the fulfillment and satisfaction of the sun.

"That sun is I, and the little lights detached from it are the creatures. And the little lights living in it are the souls that live in my Will. Have you understood now?" And I: "I believe so." But who could express what I understood? I would have rather not written anything, but the FIAT of my Jesus wanted it. May He be forever blessed.

January 29, 1919

In the Third Renovation, Jesus Will Manifest What His Divinity Did within His Humanity.

I had been adoring the wounds of Blessed Jesus and was finishing with the "Credo" (Creed). I intended to pray it within the immensity of the Divine Will, because therein one finds all the past, present and future acts of creatures, including those acts that creatures should have done, yet, due to carelessness or evil intent, did not. So I said: "Jesus, my Love, I enter into your Will because with this "Credo" I intend to reconstruct and make reparation for all the acts of faith that creatures have failed to do, all the incredulities, and the lack of adoration due to God as Creator..."

As I said these and other things, I felt my intelligence become lost in the Divine Will; and a light inundated my awareness. Within this light I discovered my sweet Jesus speaking to me again and again... but, who can say everything? I would say it confusedly. Besides I feel such repugnance at speaking about these things. If my submission to obedience were not so severe, but rather more indulgent, it wouldn't oblige me to make certain sacrifices. But You, my Life, give me strength. Don't abandon this poor ignorant one to her own devices.

Jesus seemed, then, to say: "My beloved daughter, I want to make known to you the order of my Providence. Every two thousand years I have renewed the world: In the first two thousand I renewed it through the Flood. In the second two thousand years I renewed it by my coming to earth and by manifesting my Humanity, from which radiated my Divinity in brief instances. Good people, and even the Saints, of this third two thousand year period have lived by the fruits of my Humanity and have enjoyed only droplets of my Divinity. Now we are nearing the end of this third two thousand year period, and there will be a third renewal. The general confusion in all things is but the preparation for this third renewal.

"In the second renewal I manifested what I did and suffered in my Humanity. But I manifested very little of what my Divinity did. In this third renewal I will be even more magnanimous with creatures. I will accomplish this renewal by manifesting what my Divinity did within my Humanity, how my Divine Will worked with my human will, how everything was brought together and integrated within Me, how I made and remade everything. Even the thoughts of each creature were made anew by Me and were sealed with my Divine Volition. My Love desires to be released and satisfied and wants to make known the excesses that my Divinity did within my Humanity on behalf of creatures. These exceed by far the excesses that My Humanity did externally. But first the earth must be purged and a large part of the present generation must be destroyed.

"This is why I speak so often to you concerning life in my Will, which I have not manifested to anyone before. At best others have known the shadow of my Will: the grace and the sweetness contained in doing my Will. But no one knows about penetrating into my Will, embracing Its Immensity, multiplying oneself with Me and penetrating everywhere, penetrating Heaven and penetrating hearts, abandoning human ways and acting in divine ways — all this while still on earth. So unknown is this living in my Will that many will consider it strange, and those who do not have their minds open to the light of Truth won't understand anything about it. But I will open a way for Myself little by little. First, I will manifest one truth, then another concerning this living in my Will, so that ultimately they will understand.

"The first link that made it truly possible to live in my Will was my Humanity. My Humanity and my Divinity swam in the Eternal Volition. They followed all the acts of creatures and appropriated them for Themselves. They gave the Father on behalf of all creatures the worth, the love and the kiss of the Eternal Volition. Within the confines of the Eternal Will I saw all the acts that creatures did, and could have done but did not do. I did those acts which had not been done and repeated those acts which had been poorly done. These acts which have been done only by Me are suspended in my Will. I await for creatures to come and live in my Will so that they can repeat in my Will all that I did.

"Now I have selected you as the second link in conjunction with my Humanity, fusing your link with Mine as you live in my Will and repeat my own acts. Were this not to occur, my Love would not find release and satisfaction in this respect. It would be lacking the glory from creatures for everything that my Divinity did in my Humanity. It would be lacking the perfect fulfillment of Creation, which needs to be enclosed and perfected within my Will. It would be as if I had shed all my Blood, had suffered so much... and no one were aware of it. Who would have loved Me? What heart would have been moved? None! Therefore, I could not have harvested in any heart the fruits of my suffering, the glory of my Redemption.

Interrupting Jesus, I said: "My Love, if there is so much good in this living in the Divine Will, why haven't You manifested it before?" He replied: "My daughter, first I had to make known what my Humanity did and suffered externally. This would dispose souls to know what my Divinity did within. Creatures are incapable of comprehending my work all at once. Therefore I manifest Myself little by little.

"Later the links of other creatures will be joined to your link united to Me. Then I will have a court full of souls living in my Will who shall repeat all the acts of creatures. I will receive the glory of having creatures repeat the acts that, because only I have done them up to now, are suspended in my Will. These acts will be repeated by creatures of varied backgrounds: virgins, Priests, lay persons, according to their callings. They will no longer act on the human plane, but will penetrate into my Will; and their acts, now all divine, will be multiplied for all creatures.

Then I will receive on behalf of all creatures divine glory for all the many times the Sacraments were received in a merely human manner, and for the other times they were received profanely, and for other receptions soiled by self-seeking; and I will receive divine glory for the many good works in which I appear more dishonored than honored. I long so much for this time... you also, pray and long for it with Me. Don't separate your link from its unity with Mine, yours being the first to begin."

February 20, 1919

Every Created Thing Is a Relation, a Channel of Grace and Love between God and the Creature.

Continuing in my usual state, Jesus said to me: "My daughter, enter into Me, into my Divinity and flow in my Eternal Will. There you shall find the Creative Power as in the act of creating the great machine of the Universe. In everything that I created, I put a relation, a channel of grace, a special Love between the Supreme Majesty and the creature. But since I already foresaw that the creature, ungratefully, would not respect these relations, these graces, and this Love, I should have suspended Creation, for its not being recognized nor appreciated. But on seeing that my Humanity would so admirably appreciate everything and that It would have It's relation with the Eternal One for everything created, that is — recognize Him and love Him, not only on its own, but for the entire human family, I did not look at the error of my children. I stretched out the sky with the greatest contentment, decking it with stars, knowing that those stars were to be so many and varied relations, graces without number, and rivers of Love which were to run between my Humanity and the Supreme Being.

"The Eternal One looked at the sky and remained content in seeing the immense harmonies and the communications of Love that I opened between Heaven and earth. Therefore I went beyond; and, with a Creative Word, I created the sun there, as the continual reporter of the Supreme Being, gifting it with light and heat, suspending it between Heaven and earth, in the act of regulating everything, of fecundating and illuminating all with its searching eye of light that seems to say to all: 'I am the most perfect preacher of the Divine Being; look at me and you will recognize Him. He is immense light; He is interminable Love; He gives life to all; He has need of nothing, and no one can touch Him. Look at me well and you shall recognize Him. I am his shadow, the reflection of his Majesty, and the demonstrator and continuous reporter of his Eternal Glory."

"Oh, what oceans of Love and relations were opened between my Humanity and the Supreme Majesty! And so, everything you see, even the smallest flower is one more bond between the creature and the Creator. This is why it was just to seek gratitude and love on the part of the creature. Then I substituted for everyone and thanked and adored the Creative Power on behalf of everyone. But my Love toward so much goodness is not content; wherefore, I would like other creatures to thank, love and adore this Creative Power, and, as far as it is possible to a creature, to participate in those relations that the Eternal One has dispersed in all the world, and in the name of all, to render homage to this Act of the Creation by the Eternal One. But do you know who can render this homage? The souls who live in my Will who, as they enter It, find as in Act all the Acts of the Supreme Majesty. And since the Divine Will is found in everything and in everyone, these acts are multiplied in everyone, and can render honor, glory, adoration, and love for everyone. Therefore, come into my Will; come with Me before the Most High, to be the first to render homage for the Creation of the whole Universe."

I do not know how I entered into this Divine Will, but I was always together with my sweet Jesus; and I saw this Supreme Majesty in the Act of issuing forth all of Creation. Oh God, how much Love! Each created thing received the seal of Love, the key of communication, the mute language of speaking eloquently of God, but to whom? To the ungrateful creature! My little intelligence lost itself in seeing so many channels of communication and the immense Love that came forth, and the creature as it were, oblivious to all these goods. Wherefore, together with Jesus, multiplying ourselves in everyone, we adored, gave thanks and recognized the Creative Power in the name of all; and the Eternal One received the glory from Creation. Jesus disappeared and I returned to myself.

February 24, 1919

Man: The Masterpiece of the Creative Power

As I was in my usual state, Blessed Jesus came to me and said: "My daughter, you haven't made any comments concerning the creation of mankind, the masterpiece of the Creative Power. In mankind the Eternal One put his Love, his Beauty, his Mastery, not in little droplets, but in waves and rivers and, in an excess of Love, He even placed Himself as the center of man. But He wanted a worthy dwelling in man. What, therefore, did this Uncreated Supreme Majesty do? He created man in his own Image and Likeness. Then from the depths of his Love He exhaled, and with his Omnipotent Breath infused life into man and gave him all his qualities, proportionate to each creature, and made of each a little 'god.'

"Everything you see in Creation is nothing compared to the creation of man. Oh! How many heavens, stars and much more beautiful suns I infused into the created soul! What variety of beautiful things, what harmonies! Suffice it to say that when He gazed upon created man the Eternal One found him so beautiful, but so beautiful that He fell in love with him. Jealous of this, his momentous creation, the Eternal One Himself became the custodian and master of man and said to him: 'I have created everything for you. I give you dominion over all; everything is yours, and you shall be all Mine. You will not be able to understand all this: the seas of Love, the intimate and exclusive relationships, and the likeness that flows between Creator and creature.'

"Oh! Daughter of my Heart! If creatures only realized how beautiful is their soul, how many divine gifts it contains, and that it surpasses all created things in beauty, power, and light! So much does a creature surpass all created things that one can call a creature a little god, a little world that contains all within himself. If he only realized this! Oh! How the creature would hold himself in the highest esteem, refusing to soil even with the slightest fault such an immense beauty, such a momentous prodigy of the Creative Power! But the creature, almost blind when it comes to knowing himself, and more than blind when it comes to knowing his Creator, soils himself with thousands of filthy acts, so that he disfigures almost completely the work of his Creator, even to the point that the creature can be recognized only with great difficulty. Think, yourself ...what sorrow do We not suffer? Therefore, come into my Will, and together with Me go before the Throne of the Eternal One. On behalf of our brothers let us render satisfaction for all the acts that creatures should do out of gratitude for his having created them in a prodigy of the Love of his Omnipotence... and for which creatures are, nevertheless, so ungrateful."

In an instant we found ourselves before the Supreme Majesty; and on behalf of all we gave love, thanksgiving and adoration for having created us with such excesses of Love, and for having gifted us with such immense and beautiful qualities.

February 27, 1919

In the Divine Will There Are No Obstacles to God's Love.

As I continue in my usual state, Blessed Jesus comes and almost always calls me into his Will to make reparation and to replace the acts of creatures with divine acts. This time He said to me: "My daughter, what a stench earth exhales. I don't find any place for Myself, and I am compelled by this stench to flee the earth. But you can make for Me some balsamic, perfumed air. Do you know how? — by doing everything you do in my Will. As you do these acts you create a divine wind. I will come to breathe it and will find a place for Myself on earth. Just as my Will circulates everywhere, so also will I feel everywhere the wind you create; and it will dispel the pestilent air that the earth sends Me."

A little while later He returned and added: "My daughter, what darkness! There is so much darkness that the earth seems to be covered with a black cloak, so dark that creatures no longer see; they are either blind or, having sight, lack sufficient light to see. I want for Myself not only divine air, but also light. Therefore let your acts in my Will be continuous. In that way you will not only produce divine air for your Jesus, but also light. You will be my reflector, a reflector of my Love and of my own Light. What's more, as you perform your acts in my Will you shall build tabernacles. And to the degree you form your thoughts, words, reparations, and acts of love within my Will, as many Hosts will issue forth from you because they will be consecrated in my Will. I will have as many tabernacles as I desire; the Hosts shall be innumerable, and in every instant we shall commune together; and I will be able to shout with all my lungs: 'Freedom, freedom! Come, everyone within my Will to enjoy true liberty!'

"How many obstacles and impediments does the soul encounter outside of my Will! But in my Will, she is free! I give her the freedom to love Me as she desires. Moreover, I say to her: 'Leave your human rags, take what is divine. I am not a miser, nor am I stingy with my goods; I want you to take everything. Love Me immensely! Here, take all my Love and make it your own; take my Power and make it yours; my Beauty... take them for your own, and the more you take the happier will your Jesus be.' Earth creates few tabernacles for Me. The Hosts can almost be counted. If you add to this the sacrileges and irreverences to which I am exposed... Oh! How offended I am, how obstructed is my Love! Within my Will, on the other hand, there are no obstacles. There isn't even the shadow of an offense; and a creature gives Me love, divine reparations and complete correspondence; and together with Me, all the evils of the entire human family are replaced. Therefore, be attentive and do not move from the point to which I call you and where I want you."

March 6, 1919

The Graces with Which Jesus Disposes a Soul to Live in the Divine Will

I was contemplating what my sweet Jesus was saying concerning the Divine Will, and I said to myself: "How is it possible that a soul can arrive so high as to live more in Heaven than on earth?"

Then Jesus came and said: "My daughter, although it is impossible for creatures, everything is possible for Me. It is truly the greatest, most prodigious act of my Omnipotence and of my Love. And when I wish, I can do anything; and acts that seem difficult are most easy for Me. Nevertheless I want a creature's "yes." I desire that the creature, as if he were soft wax, submit to everything I wish to make of him. Furthermore, rather than calling a creature to live entirely in my Will all at once, I begin by calling him into my Will only occasionally. I strip him of everything, and I subject him to a judgment of sorts. This is because in my Will there are no judgments. Everything is affirmed in Me. There is only judgment outside of my Will. Who would dare judge anything that is within my Will? To be sure, I never judge Myself.

Many times I take a creature to the point of death, even physical death; then I bring him back to life. Then the soul lives as if she were no longer alive. With her heart in Heaven, her greatest martyrdom is to have to live on earth. How many times have I not done this with you? These are all graces given to dispose the soul to live in my Will. Have I not repeatedly bound you with the chains of my graces, of my many visits? The purpose of all this is to make you suited to live in the immense ocean of my Will. Therefore don't try to investigate. Just continue soaring high in my Will."

May 22, 1919

In the <u>Era of Life in the</u> Divine Will, Souls Shall Complete the Glory of Creation by Living in the Divine Will.

As I continued in my usual state, my little mind became lost in the Holy Will of God and, though unaware of how I acquired this knowledge, I understood that creatures don't give God the glory that they should give Him. This made me feel distressed. Then my sweet Jesus, desiring to instruct and console me, by enlightening my intellect said: "My daughter, all of my works are complete. Therefore, all the glory that creatures should give Me will be completely given. Creation will not see its last day until all of creation gives Me the honor and glory desired and ordained by Me. What some creatures fail to give Me, I take from others, in whom I double my grace. Because I give these latter the grace which others reject, I receive from them twice the love and glory. To some creatures I give the graces that I would otherwise give to ten, to some the graces destined for one hundred, to some those destined for one thousand, according to their disposition to receive these graces. Sometimes I give a creature the graces destined for a city, or a province, or even entire kingdoms. Then they love Me and give Me the glory I should have received from ten, from one hundred, or from one thousand. That is how the glory due Me from creation is completed.

"When I see that a creature cannot receive more grace, even though it is willing, I draw him towards my Will; and there he finds the virtue of being able to multiply a single act into as many acts as he desires, thereby giving Me the glory, the honor and the love that other creatures fail to give Me. Therefore, I am preparing the *Era of Living in my Will*. What the past generations have not done and those in the future will not do, the good souls in this *Era of my Will* will do. They shall complete the love, the glory and the honor which all creation owes Me; and I will give them astounding and unheard-of graces.

"That is why I call you into my Will, and I whisper in your ear: *'Jesus, I place at your feet the adoration and recognition of the entire human family. I place in your heart a kiss from all. On your lips I place my kiss, and with this kiss I consummate the kiss of all generations. With my arms I embrace you, so as to embrace you with the arms of all creatures, to offer and give You the glory of all creatures and of all their acts and works.'* Then I feel in you, and receive from you, the adoration, the 'I love You!', the kiss, etc. from all the human family. How then can I help but give you the love, the kisses and the graces that I should give to all other creatures.

"You should know, my daughter, that creatures, through their acts on earth, create the wealth that they shall enjoy in Heaven. He who does little, shall have little wealth in Heaven. He who does much, shall have much in Heaven. If a soul has loved and glorified as much as ten souls should have, she will have tenfold happiness, a correspondingly greater amount of glory, and will be loved by Me ten times as much. If another soul has loved and glorified Me as much as one hundred souls, or one thousand souls should have, she will enjoy the delights, love and glory of one hundred or one thousand souls. Thus, I will give Creation what I have decided to give; and Creation will give Me everything I should receive from it; and my Glory shall be complete in every way."

December 6, 1919

A Soul in the Divine Will Gives God the Love that Lost Souls Will Not Give. God Made Man Free so that Man Would Do Good.

I feel I don't have the strength to express my painful grief in writing. Even so, though I did not intend to, I will write a few words that my sweet Jesus said to me because, reproaching me one day, He made me decide to write them. I remember one night I was adoring my crucified Jesus and was saying to Him:

"My Love, in your Will I find all generations; and on behalf of the entire human family I adore You, I kiss You, and I make reparation for all. I give your Wounds and your Blood to all, so that all will find their salvation. Although the lost souls can't receive any benefits from your most Holy Blood, nor can they love You, in their place I take your Blood and do what they should do. I do not want your Love to be disappointed by creatures in any way. On behalf of all I want to respond, to make reparation, to love You, to adore You... from the first man to the last that will exist.."

As I said this, my sweet Jesus extended his arms towards me and said: "My daughter, echo of my Life, as you did this my Mercy grew ever sweeter, and my Justice lost its edge, not only in the present but also in the future, because your prayer remains as a continuously ongoing act in my Will. My Mercy, having been sweetened by your prayer, will flow more abundantly; and my Justice will be less rigorous. Furthermore, I will hear from you the melody of love that I should be hearing from the souls of the lost. Then my Heart shall feel towards you an especially tender love as it finds in you the love that lost souls should be giving me, and I will pour into you all the graces that I had prepared for those souls."

Another day He said: "My daughter, let Me show you how much I love creatures. When I created the heavens, the stars, the sun and all of nature, I did not give these things any freedom. Therefore, the heavens cannot voluntarily add or remove one single star; the sun cannot voluntarily add or extinguish one single ray of light. When I created man, on the other hand, I made him free. Not only did I make him free, but I also wanted him to participate with Me in the creation of the stars, the sky, etc., in order to embellish them with the heavens of man's soul. As man did more and more good, and as man practiced virtues, I would give him the power to create, in the heaven of his soul, the stars and the most splendid of suns. And the more good he did, the more stars would be created. The greater the intensity of his love and sacrifices, the greater the splendor and intensity of light with which these suns would shine.

"And as I walked with man in the heaven of his soul, I would say to his soul: 'My child, the more you want to embellish yourself, the more you please Me. I love your beauty so much that I Myself teach you and motivate you; and when you are willing, I come running to you; and together with you I renew the Creative Power within you and give you the power to do all the good that you wish to do. I love you so much that I have not made you a slave but rather have made you free. But, woe is Me! How you have abused the power I gave you. You have the insolence to turn it into your own ruin and into an offense against your Creator!

December 26, 1919

Living in the Divine Will is a Sacrament and Surpasses, in a Wondrous Manner, All the Other Sacraments Put Together.

I was thinking to myself: "How can it be that living in the Will of God surpasses the Sacraments themselves?" when, Jesus, moving within me, said: "My daughter, why are the Sacraments called Sacraments? Because they are sacred and have the worth and power of conferring Grace and Sanctity. But these Sacraments work according to the disposition of creatures. Thus many times these Sacraments are totally unfruitful and are unable to confer the benefits they contain.

My Will, on the other hand, is Sacred and Holy and contains within Itself all the virtues of all the Sacraments together. Moreover, my Will does not have to work to make a soul disposed to receive all the benefits that It contains because, as soon as a soul is disposed to do my Will, she has already disposed herself to receive all the benefits that my Will contains. Finding the soul thus prepared and well disposed to receive It, even at the expense of the greatest sacrifice, my Will without delay communicates with the soul and pours into her all the benefits It contains.

In this manner my Will forms heroes, Martyrs of the Divine Will: the most unheard-of wonders. Besides, what do the Sacraments do but unite a soul with God? What does it mean to do my Will? Isn't it a union of the creature's will with his Creator, to lose oneself in the Eternal Will? Isn't it the nothing ascending to the All, and the All descending into the nothingness of the creature? Isn't it the most noble, most divine, purest, most beautiful, most heroic act that a soul can do? Ah, I repeat and I confirm to you that my Will is Sacrament and surpasses all the Sacraments together in a way that is much more admirable, since It needs no one's intervention nor anything material. The Sacrament of my Will is formed between my Will and the will of a soul. When both wills melt into each other they form the Sacrament. My Will is Life, and the soul who is disposed to receive Life is holy and receives Holiness, is strong and receives Fortitude, and likewise everything else.

My other Sacraments, however, must be accompanied by much effort to dispose souls to receive their benefits... and this is not always a successful effort. How many times are these channels that I have left to my Church abused, despised, trampled upon? Some even use these Sacraments the more to dirty themselves; others are placed in opposition to Me and offend Me because of the Sacraments. Ah, my daughter, if you knew the enormous sacrileges that are committed in the Sacrament of Confession... and the horrendous abuses committed in the Sacrament of the Eucharist, the immense sorrow would cause you to cry together with Me. Ah, yes, only the Sacrament of my Will can cry victory and glory; only It is complete in Its effects and, being intangible, cannot be offended by creatures. To enter into my Will a creature must leave his will and his passions. Only then does my Will lower Itself to the creature, penetrate him, fuse with him, and work Its marvels within him.

That is why, when I speak of my Will united to the will of the creature, I engage in a never-ending festival. My joy is complete, and no bitterness can come between Me and the soul. When it comes to the other Sacraments, on the other hand, my Heart swims in a sea of pain — pain caused by man's transforming them into sources of bitterness, whereas I have given them to man as sources of Grace."

May 24, 1920

Acts Done in the Divine Will Embrace All Centuries and Remain Active throughout All Eternity.

As I continued in my usual state, my ever amiable Jesus said to Me: "My daughter, acts done in my Will lose their human quality. They fuse with my divine acts and, ascending into Heaven, they disseminate everywhere, embracing all centuries, all points and all creatures. Because they are embedded within my Will, these acts are the defenders of my Throne and will make reparation for any offense that creatures commit against Me, not only in the present but until the end of time. Acts done in my Will have the power to multiply themselves according to the demands of my glory in each particular circumstance. How great the joy of a soul when, once in Heaven, she sees her acts done in my Will as they defend my Throne; and, with their continuous echo of reparation, repulse the echo of offenses coming from the earth.

"That is why in Heaven the glory of souls that have lived in my Will on earth will be different from the other Blessed. These latter will derive all their joy from Me, but the former will not only derive joy from Me, but also will have their own small rivers of joy within the sea of my joy. They will have formed these rivers while living within my sea on earth. Therefore, it is only fair that they also have them in Heaven to flow over all the Blessed.

"Oh, how beautiful these rivers are in the infinite sea of my Will. They pour themselves into Me and I into them. It will be an enthralling sight to see, before which all the Blessed will stand in awe!"

May 28, 1920

Acts Done in the Divine Will Enter into Eternity and Have Supremacy over All Human Acts.

Together with Jesus, I was offering myself in the Holy Sacrifice of the Mass so that I could undergo his same Consecration. Then, moving within me, He said: "My daughter, enter into my Will so that I can find you in all the Hosts, not only in those that have existed in the past, but also in the present and future Hosts. Then you will undergo as many Consecrations as I undergo. In every Host I place my Life, and I desire correspondence with another life. But how many fail to give me their life! They receive Me, and I give Myself to them; but they don't give themselves to Me, and my Love is offended, blocked, suffocated and unrequited. For this reason I ask you to come into my Will to undergo all the Consecrations that I undergo, so that in every Host I will find your life given in response to Mine. This will occur, not only while you are alive, but even when you are in Heaven. Having consecrated yourself in advance in my Will while on earth, you will suffer with Me even unto my last Consecration, and I will find your life being given in response to Mine until the last day."

Later He added: "Acts done in my Will are always the first among all acts, and have supremacy over them all because, having been done in my Will, they enter into the scope of Eternity. Taking their place of primacy there, they always rush to the forefront, leaving behind all human acts. It does not matter whether the acts were done earlier or later, in one epoch or another, whether they were small or great. It suffices that they were done in my Will to make them always first, so that they rush ahead of all human acts.

"Oil is a good example of this. When placed together with other edibles, even though these may be of greater value, as much as gold or silver, or of greater concentration, they all remain on the bottom; and the oil rises above them. Oil never remains on the bottom; no matter how small in amount. With its subtle reflections of light it seems to say: 'I am here to be first, above all things; I do not mix with these other things, nor do I have anything in common with them.' So it is that acts done according to my Desire, since they are done in my Will, are converted into light, light that is bound and fused with the Eternal Light. Therefore, they do not mix with human acts. What is more, acting in my Will has the power to transform human acts into divine acts. Because of this transformation, acts done in my

Will leave all other acts far behind. They take first place among all acts."

January 5, 1921

Living in the Divine Will Is the Formation of Our Life within the Life of Jesus.

As I continued in my usual state, I prayed and formulated my intention of entering into the Divine Will, thereby taking possession of all that the Divine Will encompasses and from which nothing escapes, neither past, present nor future. In the Divine will I made of myself a crown including my love, reparation, etc., and, in the name of all creatures, presented my homage before the Divine Majesty.

Then my ever amiable Jesus moved within me and said: "My daughter, the life of a soul, when lived in my Will, is truly nothing other than the formation of her life within Mine. I imprint my own form on everything that the soul does. In my Will I did nothing other than give flight to all the internal and external acts I did. I put in flight each thought of my mind, which, flying over each thought of creature, made a crown of every human intelligence. And I presented in homage before the Majesty of the Father the adoration, the glory, the love, the reparation for every created thought. I repeated this process with my glances, my words, my movements, my heartbeats, my steps. In order to live her life in my Will, the soul must respond by molding her mind into the shape of my Mind, molding her glances into the form of Mine, her words, her movements, her heartbeats, and her steps into the form of Mine. As she does this, she loses her own form and acquires Mine, subjecting the human being to repeated deaths, while giving continuous life to the Divine Will. Thus the soul will be able to enthrone in herself the Divine Life of my Will; and when this prodigious accomplishment is fully realized, her form will be fully modeled after Me.

"Only my Immense, Eternal Will finds everything: past, present, future; then reduces it to a single point, and in this point encounters all hearts beating, all minds living and all my works as ongoing acts. When a soul makes my Will her own, she does everything; she makes reparation for all, loves for all and benefits each and every one as if all were one.

"Who can ever achieve this much on his own? No virtue, no heroism, no martyrdom is comparable to my Will. They fall short in comparison to acting in my Will. Therefore, be attentive and see to it that the mission of my Will be completely fulfilled in you."

January 7, 1921

Jesus' Smile When He Sees His First Fruits: Those Souls Who by Living in the Divine Fiat, Will Return Everything to Their First State.

Finding myself in my usual state, my ever lovable Jesus came and put one of his arms around my neck. Then, approaching my heart, He took his Heart and, bringing It to mine, squeezed It together with mine. Rivers of milk flowed from his Heart, and with those rivers He filled my heart, then said:

"My daughter, see how much I love you. I have wanted to fill your heart with the milk of Grace and Love, so that all you say and do will be nothing other than the release of the Grace with which I have filled you. You will do nothing on your own. You will but place your volition in my Will, and I will do everything. You will be but the sound of my voice, the bearer of my Will, the one who will take the virtues in their human mode and make them revive in a divine mode, sealed in an eternal point which is immense, infinite..."

Having said this, He disappeared. A little later He returned. I was feeling totally annihilated upon contemplating certain things that need not be mentioned here. My affliction was extreme as I said to myself: 'Is it possible that this be happening? Ah, Jesus, don't allow it! Perhaps it is the willingness to undergo this sacrifice that you desire, but not the sacrifice itself. Besides, in this difficult state in which I find myself, I aspire to nothing but Heaven.'

Jesus, coming from within my interior, began sobbing. I felt this sobbing reverberate everywhere: in Heaven and on earth. When it was concluded, the sobbing was transformed into a smile. Just as had the sobs, this smile reverberated in Heaven and on earth. I was enthralled, and my sweet Jesus said to me: "Dear daughter of Mine, creatures inflict so much pain on Me in these sad times that they make Me weep. Being the weeping of none other than God, it reverberates in Heaven and on earth. But this pain will be replaced by a smile that will fill Heaven and earth with happiness, a smile which will appear on my lips when I see my first fruits: the children of my Will, no longer living in a human environment, but rather in one that is divine. I will see them all sealed with the seal of the Eternal Volition, Immense, Infinite. I will see that Eternal Point, that now has life only in Heaven, flow towards earth to mold the souls on earth with its infinite principles, with its Divine Behavior, with the multiplication of acts within one, single act. Just as Creation emerged from the FIAT so also, in the FIAT, it will be completed. Thus, only the children of my Will in my FIAT will complete everything; and in my FIAT living in them, I will have love, glory, reparations, thanksgiving, etc. that are complete, from all and on behalf of all.

"My daughter, all things will return to where they came from. Everything came from the FIAT, and in the FIAT everything will return to Me. The children of my Will shall be few, but in my FIAT they will give Me everything."

January 10, 1921

The "Fiat Mihi" (Let It Be Done to Me) of the Most Holy Virgin in the Divine Will, and Luisa's Fiat

I was considering what was written in the previous chapter and saying to myself: "What can Jesus want from me? If He knows what a bad person I am, that I am good for nothing..." Then Jesus, moving within me, said: "My daughter, remember that many years ago I asked you if you wanted to live in my Will, and I had you pronounce your 'Yes" within my own Will. That "Yes" was bound to an Eternal Point and to a Volition that will never end, that is in the center of my Will surrounded by an immense infinity. Were it to desire to leave there, it would not find a way. That is why I laugh and amuse Myself with your little resistance and dissatisfaction. I see you as one who by her own will is bound to the bottom of an ocean, one who, desiring to exit, finds nothing but water all around. Finally, coming to the realization that she is at the bottom of an ocean, and wanting to be rid of the desire to flee, this person casts herself even deeper into the ocean. So I, seeing you upset, as if you desired to exit but couldn't, bound as you are by your own 'Yes', laugh and amuse Myself as you cast yourself deeper into my Will. Besides, do you think it is comfortable to exit from within my

Will? You would emerge from an Eternal Point and would shake with terror!"

Later Jesus added: "I asked my beloved Mother for the first "Yes" in my FIAT and... Oh, the power of her *Fiat* in my Will! When the Divine FIAT encountered my Mother's *Fiat* they became as one and my FIAT elevated Her, made Her divine and covered Her so that without any human action She conceived Me, the Son of God. Only in my FIAT could She have conceived Me. To Her my FIAT communicated Immensity, Infinity and Fecundity in a divine way, and I was able to be conceived within Her — I, the Immense, the Eternal, the Infinite.

No sooner had She said *Fiat Mihi* (let it be done to me) than She not only possessed Me, but also possessed all creatures and all created things. She felt the lives of all creatures within Herself, and She began to be the Mother and Queen of all creatures and all things. Oh, how many wonders are contained within that 'Yes' of my Mother. If I wished to tell you about them all there would be no end to your listening! Now I have asked from you the second 'Yes' in my Will; and you, though with trepidation, pronounced it. Now this 'Yes' in my Will shall also have its portents. It will have a divine conception. Follow Me and penetrate deeper into the immense ocean of my Will, and I will take care of all the rest. My Mother did not give thought to how She would conceive Me within Herself. She merely said: *Fiat Mihi* and I took care of how She would conceive Me. You shall behave in the same manner."

January 17, 1921

The Creative Power of the Fiat in Creation. The "Fiat Mihi" of the Most Holy Virgin in the Redemption. The Fulfillment of the "Fiat Voluntas Tua" on Earth As in Heaven.

I felt my poor mind submerged in the immense ocean of the Divine Will. Everywhere I saw the seal and stamp of the FIAT. I saw it in the sun, and it seemed that the echo of the FIAT in the sun brought to me the Divine Love which darted and wounded me. And I, on the same wings as the FIAT in the sun, ascended to the Eternal One and brought love in the name of the entire human family which darted and wounded the Supreme Majesty saying: "In your FIAT You have given me all this Love, and only in the FIAT can I return it to You."

I looked at the stars, and this FIAT was also visible in them. And this FIAT brought me sweet love in its gentle and delicate splendor, hidden love, love of compassion in the midst of the night of guilt. In the FIAT, within the stars, I bore before the throne of the Eternal One, on behalf of all, the tranquil love that was to establish peace between Heaven and earth, the sweet love in the souls of those who love, the concealed love of so many others; in brief, the love of creatures as they return to God, having been freed from guilt.

But how can I say everything that I understood and did in so many FIATs in which I saw all of creation absorbed? If I wished to relate all these things I would go on too long! Then my sweet Jesus took my hands within his and, grasping them firmly, said to me:

"My daughter, the FIAT is full of Life; rather, It is Life. That is why all lives and all things emerge from within the FIAT. From my FIAT came Creation. That is why in all created things one sees the seal and stamp of the FIAT. From the *Fiat Mihi* of my beloved Mother, uttered within my Will, thereby having the same power as my FIAT of Creation, came the Redemption. Thus there is no part of the Redemption that does not bear the seal of the *Fiat Mihi* of my Mother. All my Humanity, my steps, my works, my words, etc. were sealed with her *Fiat Mihi*. My sorrows, my wounds, the thorns, the Cross, the Blood, everything carried this seal because all things bear the seal and stamp of their origin. My origin in time was the *Fiat Mihi* of my Immaculate Mother. Therefore everything I did bears this seal. Her *Fiat Mihi* is in every Sacramental Host. If mankind emerges from guilt, if a newborn is baptized, if Heaven opens its doors to receive anyone, it is the *Fiat Mihi* of my Mother which seals, which places its stamp, which accompanies everything and makes provision for all. Oh, Power of the FIAT! It surges continually, every moment; It multiplies Itself and makes of Itself the life of all good things.

"Now I wish to tell you why I asked you for your *Fiat*, your 'Yes' in my Will. It is because of the prayer that I taught: the **'Fiat Voluntas Tua Sicut In Coelo Et In Terra' (Thy Will Be Done On Earth As It Is In Heaven),** the prayer of so many centuries and so many generations. I want it now to be fulfilled. This is why I desire another 'Yes' in my Will, another *Fiat* to surge forth continually at every instant, to be multiplied to everyone. I desire that my same FIAT in a soul rise to my Throne and with my FIAT's Creative Power bring Life to earth in the: 'Your Will be done (FIAT) on earth as It is in Heaven."

Surprised and annihilated upon hearing all this, I said to Him: "Jesus, what can I say? You know how evil I am, and how inept I am at everything." He replied: "My daughter, I

116

usually elect the smallest, the poorest and most inept souls for my greatest works. There was nothing extraordinary about the external life of my own Mother — no miracles, no sign to distinguish Her from other women. Her only distinction was her perfect virtue, which drew the attention of very few. Although I gave the other Saints the distinction of performing miracles, even adorning some with My wounds, I gave my Mother nothing, nothing. Yet She was the portent of portents, the miracle of miracles, the true and perfect crucified. There is no one else like Her.

"I have the habit of acting like a master who has two servants: one is muscular and appears like a giant and is capable of anything. The other is small, weak, and inept. The latter seems incapable of doing anything important. And if the master keeps him it is more out of charity than for any other reason. Needing to send a very large sum of money somewhere — what does the master do? He calls the small servant, the inept one, and entrusts to him the large sum of money, saying to himself: 'If I entrust it to the giant he will draw everyone's attention. Thieves will assault him and steal the money. Even if he tries to defend himself with his Herculean strength he may be injured. I know he is courageous, but I want to protect him, I don't want to expose him to this evident danger. This little one, on the other hand, seeming to be inept, will draw no one's attention. No one will think that I would entrust him with such a large sum of money, so he will return safe and sound.'

"The small, inept one is surprised that his master entrusts this mission to him when he has the giant at his disposal. Trembling and full of humility, he delivers the large sum of money without anyone deigning to even glance at him, and returns safe and sound to his master, even more tremulous and humble than before. This is the way I act. The greater the work I wish to accomplish, the more I choose souls that are small, poor, ignorant, with nothing noteworthy about them. Their small status serves as a sure custodian of my work. The thieves of self-esteem and self-love, recognizing the soul's ineptitude, will pay such souls little heed. And such a soul, humble and tremulous, will carry out the mission entrusted to her by Me, recognizing that it is not herself, but I who have done everything in her."

January 24, 1921

Just As the 'Fiat' of the Creation and the 'Fiat' of the Redemption Originated in One Creature So Also the 'Fiat Voluntas Tua.'

I felt annihilated as I reflected upon this blessed FIAT, and my ever lovable Jesus chose to increase my confusion. It seems that He wants to play a game with me. While He proposes astounding and almost incredible things to me, he takes pleasure in seeing me confused and even more annihilated. But what is worse, the greatest torment of all, is that I find myself obligated by obedience to put them in writing. Then, as He rested his Head on mine, a light emanated from his Forehead towards mine, and He said to me:

"My daughter, the First FIAT was uttered in the Creation without the participation of any creature. I chose my Mother for the fulfillment of the Second FIAT. Now, to achieve its fulfillment, I wish to utter the Third FIAT. This FIAT will complete the glory and the honor of the FIAT of Creation and represents the complete fruition of the fruits of the FIAT of Redemption. These three FIATs will reflect the Sacrosanct Trinity on earth, and then I will have the **'Fiat Voluntas Tua' (Thy Will Be Done)** on earth as It is in Heaven. These three FIATs will be inseparable. One shall be the life of the other; they shall be One and Triune, yet different from one another. My Love so desires it and my glory demands it. Having sent forth from the bosom of my Creative Power the first two FIATs, I wish to emit the Third FIAT, since I cannot contain my Love any longer. This will complete the work that poured forth from Me. Otherwise, the work of Creation as well as Redemption would remain incomplete."

As I heard this I was not only confused, but also dumb-founded and said to myself: "Is all this possible? There are so many others! If He has chosen me it seems to be an act of mad-ness on Jesus' part. Besides, what could I do or say, bedridden as I am and totally inept in every sense of the word. Could I measure up to the multiplicity and infinity of the FIATs of Creation and Redemption? Since my *Fiat* is similar to these other two FIATs I must flow together with Them, do the good that They do and intertwine myself with Them. Ah, Jesus, re-consider what you are doing. I am not up to so much!"

Who can say all the foolishness that I uttered? But then my sweet Jesus returned and said to me: "Calm down, my daughter! I choose whom I wish. Be aware that I initiate all my works to-gether with a single creature, and then they become widespread. As a matter of fact, who was the first spectator of the FIAT of the Creation? — Adam, and later Eve. There was not a multi-tude of peoples. In the case of the Second FIAT the only specta-tor was my Mother. Not even St. Joseph knew anything. My Mother was more or less in your same situation. The grandeur of the creative force of my work which She felt within Herself was so great that She did not, because of her confusion, have the strength to utter a single word to anyone. Later, St. Joseph learned of it only because I Myself manifested it to him. And in such manner did this FIAT germinate within her virginal bosom as a seed, and the shoot was formed to multiply it. And later the shoot pushed forth into the daylight. But who were the spectators? Very few! In the residence in Nazareth, there were only my beloved Mother and St. Joseph. Then, as my Humanity grew, I emerged and made Myself known to a few, then to more, and now yet to even more. So will it be with the Third FIAT. It will germinate in you; the shoot will form with only the Priest knowing of it, then a few souls; then later it will spread and take the same path as Creation and Redemption. The more annihilated you feel, the more the shoot of the Third FIAT will grow in you and come to fruition. Therefore, be attentive."

February 2, 1921

The Creative Power Is in the Divine Fiat. This Is Why the Three Fiats Have the Same Worth and Power.

Continuing in my usual state, I was fusing myself with the Divine Will and saying: "My sweet Jesus, I want to love You. But I want to love you with so much love that I provide the love of all human generations that have ever existed and that shall ever be. But who can give me enough love to love You on behalf of all? It is in your Will, my Love, in which resides the Creative Power to provide and exceed the love of all and to provide and exceed everything that creatures are obligated to give to God, our Creator."

No sooner had I uttered these words, than I said: "How many foolish things am I saying!" Then my sweet Jesus, moving within me said: "My daughter, it is true; in my Will resides the Creative Power. From within a single FIAT billions of stars emerged. From the *Fiat Mihi* of my Mother, from which my Redemption originated, emerge billions and billions of acts of Grace which are communicated to souls. These acts of Grace are much more beautiful, more resplendent, and take many more different forms than the stars. Though the stars are fixed and do not reproduce themselves, acts of Grace multiply themselves infinitely. They flow at every instant and give their breath to creatures, make creatures happy, strengthen them and give them Life. Ah, if creatures could only see the supernatural dimension of Grace! They would see such a spectacle and hear such harmonies that they would think themselves to be already in Paradise!

And now the Third FIAT must also flow, together with the other two FIATS. It must multiply itself infinitely and in every instant. It must do as many acts as there are acts of Grace emerging from my bosom, as there are stars, as there are drops of water, and as there are created things brought forth by the FIAT of Creation. This Third FIAT must blend with the Others and say: 'For as many acts as you do, so many do I.'

"These three FIATs have the same worth and power. You disappear, and it is the FIAT which acts. For this reason, you too can say in my Omnipotent FIAT: 'I want to create so much love, so many prayers, so many blessings and so much glory for my God that I compensate for everyone and everything.' Your acts will fill Heaven and earth. They will replicate themselves together with the acts of Creation and Redemption, and all three sets of acts will become as one. All this may appear to be surprising and incredible to some, but only if they doubt my Creative Power. It is I who desire this, I who give this power. This should put all doubt to rest. Or am I not free to do what I Will and give to whom I wish? You have but to be attentive. I will be with you; I will provide you with my Creative Power, and I will fulfill what I desire in you."

February 8, 1921

As Creatures Become More Perverse, God Prepares the New Era of the "Fiat Voluntas Tua."

This morning, after receiving Holy Communion, I heard my ever lovable Jesus say within me: "Oh, iniquitous world, you are doing all you can to cast Me from the face of the earth, to expel Me from society, from schools, from conversations, and from everything. You are scheming to destroy temples and altars, to destroy my Church and kill my ministers. Yet, I am preparing for you an era of Love, the **Era Of My Third Fiat!** You will continue your efforts to banish Me, but I will confound you with Love. I will follow you from behind, I will appear ahead of you, to confound you with Love; and wherever you cast Me, there will I establish my Throne; and there will I reign even more than before, and in a much more astounding manner, so much so, that you yourself, will fall at the foot of my Throne, as if bound by the force of my Love."

Later He added: "Ah, my daughter, creatures become ever more perverse in evil! How many ruinous artifacts are they not preparing? They will go to such lengths as to exhaust evil itself. Yet, while creatures are engaged in following their own way, I will see to it that my **Fiat Voluntas Tua** is heard and achieves its fulfillment, that my Will reign on earth in an entirely new way. I will go about preparing the **Era Of The Third Fiat** in which my Love will find release in a manner both marvelous and unprecedented.

Ah yes, I want to totally confound man with Love. Therefore, be attentive. I want you next to Me preparing this Era of Divine, Celestial Love. Let us work together!" Then, approaching my mouth, He infused into me his omnipotent FIAT; and I received a new Life, whereupon Jesus disappeared.

February 16, 1921

To Enter into the Divine Will, It Is Enough that a Soul Desire It and Give Up Its Own Will.

As I reflected upon the Holy Divine Will my sweet Jesus said to me: "My daughter, you don't need paths, nor doors, nor keys, to enter into my Will because my Will can be found everywhere. It flows under one's feet, to the right, to the left, over one's head — everywhere. To enter, creatures need but remove the pebble of their own will. Although it lies within my Will, their will does not participate nor enjoy Its effects. It is alien to my Will because that pebble, a soul's own will, hinders the flow of my Will, just as the rocks on a beach keep the ocean water from flowing everywhere. But if a soul removes the rock of her own will, in that very same instant she flows in Me and I in her; and she finds all My goods at her disposal: power, light, assistance and everything she desires. That is why there are no special paths, nor doors, nor keys to my Will. A soul has but to desire it and all is done. My Will assumes all the work, gives the soul what she lacks, and makes her expand into all the limitless boundaries of my Will. With virtues it is just the opposite. How many efforts are needed, how many battles, how many long paths... and when it seems that some virtue smiles on a soul, a somewhat violent passion, a temptation, a frustration or an unexpected encounter casts the soul backwards, back to the starting point, where she must start anew at the beginning of the road."

February 22, 1921

The Third Fiat Will Make Man Return to His Original State. God Will Find Repose in His Completed Work.

I was in my usual state; and my sweet Jesus was silent, so I said to Him: "My Love, why don't you speak to me? Why don't you say something to me?" Then Jesus said: "My daughter, it is my custom to maintain a period of silence after I speak. I wish to repose in my own word, that is, in my own act, emanated from within Myself. I did this in Creation. I said: 'FIAT LUX,' and the light emerged from Me. I said FIAT to all other things, and they emerged from Me. Then I wished to repose, so my Eternal Light rested in the light which emerged from Me into time. My Love rested itself in the love with which I imbued all that was created. My Beauty reposed in the beauty with which I endowed the Universe. In like manner reposed my Wisdom and Power, which I had used to order everything with such a degree of wisdom and power that, upon beholding everything, I Myself said: 'How beautiful is the work that has sprung forth from Me; I want to repose in it. I act in this same way with a soul. After speaking to her, I like to repose and enjoy the effects of my word."

Later He added: "Let us utter a 'FIAT' together." Then everything: Heaven and earth were filled with adoration to the Supreme Majesty. Again He repeated: "FIAT," and the Blood, the Wounds, the Sorrows of Jesus emerged and multiplied themselves infinitely. A third time: "FIAT," and this FIAT multiplied itself in all the wills of creatures, and sanctified them.

Then He said: "My daughter, these three FIATS are the Creative, the Redemptive and the Sanctifying. When I created man I endowed him with three powers: intelligence, memory and will. With three FIATs I will complete the work of sanctification in man. The intelligence of man is enraptured by the Creative FIAT. How many things about Me man comes to understand. He becomes aware of how I love him through my hidden Presence in all created things, so that he can come to know Me; and thereby I give him Love with which to love Me in return. The FIAT of Redemption binds the memory of man with the boundlessness of my Love, which led Me to suffer so much to help man and save him from the state of guilt. In the Third FIAT my Love desires an even greater release for itself. I want to assault the human will. I want my own Will to act as the support of the human will, so that the human will shall not only be enraptured, nor merely bound, but also sustained by an Eternal Will, a Will which, taking advantage of these other supports, will almost be inescapable for man.

The generations will not cease until my Will reigns on earth. My Redemptive FIAT will interpose itself between the Creative FIAT and the Sanctifying FIAT. They will entwine, all three together, and bring to fulfillment the sanctification of man. The Third FIAT will give creatures such grace that they will return almost to their original state. Only when I have seen man as he emerged from Me, will my work be complete. Then will I enjoy perpetual repose in this, my last FIAT. Only the Life of my Will shall return man anew to his original state. Therefore, be attentive and, together with Me, help Me accomplish the sanctification of creatures."

Upon hearing all this, I said: "Jesus, my Love, I don't know how to do what You do, not even after you teach me; and I am almost afraid of the reproaches You will give me when I don't do well what You ask of me."

125

Then He, all goodness, said: "I, too, know that you cannot do perfectly what I tell you. Therefore, I will supply for you what you cannot attain. But it is necessary that you take heart and comprehend what you are to do, being fully aware that if you cannot do it all, you will at least do what you can. Be aware that when I speak, your will is bound to Mine; and you desire to do what I tell you. That way I accept what you do as if you had done it all."

I replied: "How will it be possible to reveal to others and teach them this mode of living in the Divine Will, and who will be disposed to do this? Jesus said: "My daughter, even if no one had been saved by my descent to the earth, in Me the task of glorifying the Father would have been complete. So now, though no one else should desire to receive this immense good, which will in fact not be the case, you alone would suffice and would give Me the complete glory that I desire to receive from all creatures."

March 2, 1921

Jesus Exchanges the Role of Victim for the Higher Role of Preparing The Kingdom of the Divine Will.

Finding me in my usual state when He came, my ever lovable Jesus said: "My daughter, the Third FIAT, my 'FIAT Voluntas Tua' (Thy Will be done on Earth as It is in Heaven) will be like the rainbow that appeared in the heavens after the Flood. As a rainbow of peace it assured mankind that the Flood had ceased. Such will be the Third FIAT. As it becomes known, both loving and disinterested souls will enter into the life of my FIAT. Like rainbows of peace, they will repacify Heaven and earth, and will cause the flood of so many sins that inundate the earth to recede. The life of these rainbows of peace will be the Third FIAT, so that my FIAT VOLUNTAS TUA will have its fulfillment in them. Just as the Second FIAT called Me to earth to live among mankind, so the Third FIAT will call down my Will to live in souls; and there It will reign on earth as It does in Heaven."

Later He added: "My daughter, arise and come into my Will. I have selected you among millions and millions so that my Will shall be completely fulfilled in you; and then, like a rainbow of peace attracting with its seven colors, you can attract others to live their lives in my Will. Let us put the earth aside. Up until this moment I have kept you close to Me to placate my justice and to keep the most severe punishments from raining down on earth. But now, let us allow the tide of human evil to flow. I want you, together with Me in my Will, to concern yourself with preparing the Hour of my Will. As you penetrate deeper along the path of My Will the rainbow of peace will form. This rainbow will be the unifying link between the Divine Will and the human will. From it my Will shall have life on earth. It will initiate the fulfillment of my prayer and that of the entire Church: "Thy Kingdom come, The Will be done on earth as It is in Heaven."

March 8, 1921

As the Most Holy Virgin Called the Word to Become Incarnate in Her Womb, So Luisa Calls the Divine Will to Live in Her on Earth.

As I prayed, I fused myself entirely with the Divine Will; and my sweet Jesus emerged from within me, placed his arm around me, and said: "My daughter, my Mother, with her love, with her prayers, and with her self-effacement, called Me from Heaven to earth to become incarnate within her womb. With your love and by losing yourself always in my Will, you will call my Will to earth to live within you; and then you will give Me life in all other creatures. Since by calling Me from Heaven to earth within her womb, my Mother did a unique act, one that will not be repeated. I enriched Her with all graces and endowed Her with such Love that She exceeds in love all creatures together. I made Her first in privileges, in glory, in everything, so much so that I can say that the Eternal One reduced all that is eternal to a single point and poured it into Her in torrents, in huge oceans, to such an extent that all creatures remain far below Her.

"When you call my Will into you, you also do a unique act. Out of respect for my Will which inhabits you, I must pour enough graces and Love into you to make you surpass all other creatures. Since my Will is supreme over all and is Eternal, Immense and Infinite, then I must communicate to, enrich and endow with the same qualities of my Will, that soul in which the Life of my Will is to have its beginning and fulfillment, giving that soul supremacy over all things. My Eternal Will shall take the past, the present and the future, reduce them to one single point and pour them into you. My Will is Eternal and desires to live wherever It encounters the eternal. My Will is Immense and

128

desires to live in Immensity, is Infinite and seeks Infinity... How can It find all this if I don't place It in you beforehand?"

Upon hearing all this I was terrified and bewildered (and if I have written this, it is because obedience has imposed itself). I then said: "Jesus, what are you saying? Do you want to confuse and humiliate me to the dust? I feel I cannot endure what you are saying, I feel a terror that totally petrifies me!"

Then Jesus added: "What I say to you will be of service to Myself. It is a requirement of the Sanctity and dignity of my Will. I do not lower Myself to dwell wherein I do not find what belongs to Me. You will be but the depositary of such a great benefit and must be zealous in guarding it. Therefore, take heart and do not fear."

March 17, 1921

Jesus Takes Luisa from the Role His Humanity Had on Earth to the Role that His Divine Will Had within His Humanity.

I was saying to my sweet Jesus: "The more You say You give me through your Holy Volition, the viler and the more evil I feel. I think it should be just the opposite, I think I should feel less evil."

Then Jesus said to me: "My daughter, the more the grain of my Will grows in you, the more you will feel the vileness of your husk. When the shaft begins to form, the grain and the husk are as one. But as the life of the shaft develops and the grain matures, the husk becomes distinguishable from the grain, serving to protect the grain. And so, the viler you feel, the more the grain of my Will is formed within you, and the closer it comes to its perfect maturity. The husk is nothing other than your weak nature, which as it lives together with the Holiness and Nobility of my Will, feels its vileness more and more."

Then He added: "My beloved, up to now you have experienced the role, assumed by Me, of my Humanity on earth. Now I want you to change roles. I want to give you one that is more noble and more comprehensive. I want to give you the role played by my Will within my Humanity. See how much higher and more sublime this new role is: my Humanity had a beginning, my Will is eternal; my Humanity is circumscribed and has limits, my Will, having no confines nor limits, is immense. I could not give you a more noble, elevated and distinguished role."

When I heard this, I said to Him: "Sweet Jesus, I cannot find any reason why You would want to give me such a great role. I have done nothing to deserve such a great favor."

Jesus replied: "The whole reason is my Love! — As well as your insignificance, your living in my arms like a baby who is concerned for nothing other than her Jesus, and the fact that you have never refused any of the sacrifices I have requested of you. I am not impressed by things that appear great, because in those things there is always much that is human. I am rather impressed by small things, things which appear insignificant but which are great in and of themselves! Besides, you should know by now that I would give you a totally special mission in my Will. Never before have I spoken with anyone constantly about my Will, nor have I ever revealed Its admirable effects. With you I have behaved like a teacher who wants his pupil to be perfect in the knowledge of medicine, or history, or of anything else. What does he do? Such a teacher seems to be unable to speak of anything else. He always speaks about that very same topic."

"Thus have I behaved with you. I have become Teacher of the Divine Will and behaved as if I were ignorant concerning every other topic. Now, having instructed you very well, I have shown you your mission and have made you aware that with you will begin the fulfillment of the **Fiat Voluntas Tua (Let Your Will Be Done)** on earth. Take courage, my daughter, I see that you are disheartened. Do not fear, my entire Will shall aid and sustain you. As He said this, with his hands He caressed my head, my face, and my heart, as if to confirm in me what He had said. Then He left."

April 2, 1921

The Soul Who Acts in the Divine Will Gives for All and Receives From All.

It seems as though my poor mind is stunned, and I cannot find words to put on paper what I feel. If my Jesus wants me to write, then He will very gently tell me with words whatever He infuses in me by way of illumination. I only remember that when He came He said:

"My daughter, I feel in that soul who in my Will prays, loves, makes reparation, kisses Me and adores Me as if all creatures prayed, loved Me, etc., because my Volition encompasses all things and all creatures in my Will. Thus such a soul gives Me the kiss, the love and the adoration of all creatures. I, finding all creatures in this soul, give to this soul all the kisses and all the love that I would like to have given to all other creatures. The soul in my Will is not happy until she sees Me fulfilled in the love of all, until she sees Me kissed and adored by all. In my Will it is impossible to do things half way, only completely; and so I cannot give small things to a soul who acts in my Will, but only things that are so immense that they will be sufficient for all creatures. With a soul who acts in my Will I behave like a person who needs the work of ten persons; but only one offers to do the work, and the rest reject it. Is it not only fair that everything I wanted to give to the ten all go to the one who worked? If this were not so, then where would be the difference between one who acts in my Will and one who acts in his own will?"

April 23, 1921

The War of Love that the Divine Will Shall Wage upon Creatures

I am spending the most bitter days. My ever lovable Jesus is almost entirely eclipsed. What sorrow! What grief! I feel my mind beyond its human limits in his Will. How I desire to take this Holy Volition and make It descend in the midst of men, and give It to each one to become their own life. My mind is stretched between the Divine Will and the human will of everyone, in order to make of them a single whole.

As I await in the greatest depths of my bitterness, my sweet Jesus has moved within me; and taking my hands in his, He said: "My daughter, take courage, I will come. Don't concern yourself with anything but my Will. Put aside the earth. Evil will become tired. It will plant terror and destruction everywhere; but the end will come, and my Love will triumph over all evil. Therefore, expand your will into Mine, and like a second heaven, with all your acts, you will extend yourself over the heads of all; and I will view the acts of creatures through your acts, which are divine because they emanate from my Will. Thus you shall force my Eternal Will to give the gifts and the graces needed before descending in the midst of creatures in order to wage a war of love against them."

Later, with grief in his voice, He added: "My daughter, it will happen with Me as with a father whose sons are so malevolent that they desist from evil only when it is impossible for them to continue. If they go so far as to desire to kill their father, it is not surprising that they kill each other over their differences. Nor is it surprising that being at the point of extinguishing each other, they do not even remember that they have a Father. What is this Father to do? Exiled by his own children as they fight each other, wound each other and are at the point of perishing from hunger, the Father sweats to acquire new riches, new gifts and remedies for his children. Thus, when He sees them almost lost, He is able to go into their midst to increase their riches, give them medicine to heal their wounds; and He brings to all of them peace and happiness. Then these children, overcome by so much Love, will become attached to their Father in a lasting peace and will love Him. This is what will happen with Me. That is why I want you in my Will as a daughter of my Will, and together with Me in the work of acquiring new riches to be given to creatures. Be faithful to Me and don't concern yourself with anything else."

* * *

This ends the English Language version of this Book. The original version in Spanish included from this point the entirety of Volumes 13 and 14 of Luisa's writings. These and other of Luisa's writings can be obtained in English as well as in Spanish from:

The Luisa Piccarreta Center
for the Divine Will
P.O. Box 5 - Ortega Station
Jacksonville, FL 32210

MONS. CARMELO CASSATI
Archbishop of Trani - Barletta - Bisceglie
Titular of Nazareth

ARCHDIOCESE of TRANI - BARLETA - BISCEGLIE

Cause of Beatification of the Servant of God, Luisa Piccarreta, Secular, Dominican Tertiary

- EDICT -

for the Collecting of the Writings

The Tribunal of the Archdiocese of Trani - Barletta - Bisceglie has begun the cognitive process about the life and virtues in general, as well as the miracles and supernatural gifts of the Servant of God, Luisa Piccarreta, secular, Dominican Tertiary; and having to collect the writings attributed to her, according to the Code of Canon Law and conforming to Norms issued by the Pontiff, John Paul II, on the 7th of February 1983, We order all those who may have been in possession of any object, and writing on any subject, which may have for author the foresaid Servant of God, to return them with due promptness to Us personally or to the Postulator of the Cause, Mons. Felice Posa, House of Divine Providence - 70052 Bisceglie (Bari) Italy.

Those who wish to retain the originals of the writings, may present duly authenticated copies.

Furthermore, We remind everyone and each of the faithful, be they ecclesiastics, religious or laity, that the Code of Canon Law directs them to give Us information on everything which may shed light on the reputation of sanctity of the foresaid Servant of God, as well as the miracles which have occurred or may occur through her intercession.

Lastly, We order that the present **Edict** be affixed on the doors of the Curia and the Parish Churches and Rectories of our Archdiocese for a period of three months, and that it be brought to the attention of the faithful in all those Dioceses in which there may be found writings of the Servant of God, in a manner which the Ordinary of the place will deem most opportune, and that he may, moreover, give this matter the maximum disclosure, even by printed means.

Given in Trani, from the See of the Curia, November 19, 1994.

Cancelliere
Mons. Giuseppe Ascian

+ Carmelo Cassati
Arcivescovo
Carmelo Cassati

Mons. CARMELO CASSATI
ARCIVESCOVO DI TRANI - BARLETTA - BISCEGLIE
TITOLARE DI NAZARETH

To whom it may concern,

In our Archdiocese of Trani-Barletta-Bisceglie the Cause of Beatification of the Servant of God Luisa Piccarretta has been initiated, and we have found, as persons worthy of our trust to gather information, objects, writings, or any other things which may be inherent to promoting this Cause, as well as monetary offerings, ONLY Mr. Thomas Fahy, residing at 4451 Iorquois Ave., Jacksonville, FL, and Mr. and Mrs. Miguel Machado, residing at 5900 Leonard Ave., Coral Gables, FL.

These persons will remain in contact with the members of the Diocesan Tribunal for the Cause of Beatification, and will render notice of all their activity to the same Tribunal.

In faith,

+ Carmelo Cassati

+Carmelo Cassati
Archbishop of Trani-Barletta-Bisceglie

Trani, November 26, 1994

*The following is a letter of endorsement from Archbishop Carata for the English language translations of the works of Luisa Piccarreta published by the **Luisa Piccarreta Center for the Divine Will.***

♦

PRESENTATION OF THE ENGLISH EDITION

The radiance of the sun is too much for our eyes, yet its light gives and maintains life in the world; its only function is to glorify. The new world which you are about to enter, as you turn these pages, are rays from the Eternal Sun which invite you to gravitate away from your human will, to return to the reality of your existence, to enter into the fullness of the light, so that you too can give light and— glorify!

I have observed how from all five continents many simple souls, so small, yet so loved by God, have happily unburdened themselves of their meager worries and petty desires to accept the investiture of our Lord's yoke, the sweet burden of the Divine Will, an all-embracing, all-loving, divinely humble chore of sharing in the uncompleted suffering of the Cross. They, as regenerated sons of God, are constantly active within the bosom of the Church, surrendering their own life to bring others into the Life of God's Kingdom.

It is awesome that such abundant fruit, maturing in nations around the world, should have come forth from such a small tree planted by God here in Corato. It gives me great satisfaction to know that Luisa is now accessible, with her wisdom and her sublime science, to the English- speaking faithful. It has become a cross-cultural spirituality, not looking for that exterior manifestation, but so readily accepted as that sorely needed inner consolation which encourages us to face this gravely lacerated world. I dare say, my dear friends, that your relationship with God is about to be redimensioned.

The present translation [see publications list], given for publication to the Luisa Piccarreta Center for the Divine Will, comes from the Italian original approved by the Ecclesiastical Tribunal for the Cause of Beatification of Luisa Piccarreta here in the diocese of Trani-Barletta-Bisceglie, and you may enjoy this spiritual masterpiece with the confidence that our much-beloved Daughter of the Divine Will, ever so faithful to obedience and the magisterium of the Church, continues, together with all of Heaven, to illuminate us as we work for the diffusion of her Writings.

May God's richest blessings abide always with both this Work and the reader.

+*Giuseppe Carata*
Archbishop Emeritus
Archdiocese of Trani-Nazareth   Corato, June 8, 1995

Archbishop Carata is the retired Archbishop of Trani, Italy, the diocese where Luisa Piccarretta lived. He is the co-founder of Association Luisa Piccarreta.

Consecration to the Divine Will

Oh adorable and Divine Will, behold me here before the immensity of Your Light, that Your eternal goodness may open to me the doors and make me enter into It to form my life all in You, Divine Will. Therefore, oh adorable Will, prostrate before Your Light, I, the least of all creatures, put myself into the little group of the sons and daughters of Your Supreme FIAT. Prostrate in my nothingness, I invoke Your Light and beg that It clothe me and eclipse all that does not pertain to You, Divine Will. It will be my Life, the center of my intelligence, the enrapturer of my heart and of my whole being. I do not want the human will to have life in this heart any longer. I will cast it away from me and thus form the new Eden of Peace, of happiness and of love. With It I shall be always happy. I shall have a singular strength and a holiness that sanctifies all things and conducts them to God.

Here prostrate, I invoke the help of the Most Holy Trinity, that They permit me to live in the cloister of the Divine Will and thus return in me the first order of creation, just as the creature was created.

Heavenly Mother, Sovereign and Queen of the Divine Fiat, take my hand and introduce me into the Light of the Divine Will. You will be my guide, my most tender Mother, and will teach me to live in and to maintain myself in the order and the bounds of the Divine Will. Heavenly Mother, I consecrate my whole being to Your Immaculate Heart. You will teach me the doctrine of the Divine Will and I will listen most attentively to Your lessons. You will cover me with Your mantle so that the infernal serpent dare not penetrate into this sacred Eden to entice me and make me fall into the maze of the human will.

Heart of my greatest Good, Jesus, You will give me Your flames that they may burn me, consume me, and feed me to form in me the Life of the Divine Will.

Saint Joseph, you will be my protector, the guardian of my heart, and will keep the keys of my will in your hands. You will keep my heart jealously and shall never give it to me again, that I may be sure of never leaving the Will of God.

My Guardian Angel, guard me; defend me; help me in everything so that my Eden may flourish and be the instrument that draws all men into the Kingdom of the Divine Will. Amen.

A comprehensive set of the writings
on the DivineWill by the Servant of God,
Luisa Piccarreta, are available in both
English and Spanish from:

**The Luisa Piccarreta Center
for the Divine Will**

P.O. Box 5 - Ortega Station
Jacksonville, FL 32210 - U.S.A.
Fax 904-389-5208